Business Organization
And
Change Management

:: Author ::

RAJESHKUMAR A. SHRIMALI
(M.COM, B.ED, UGC NET, M.PHIL)

Published By

Green Flag Foundation
Sabarkantha, Gujrat-383210, India.
www.eternityzxy.com

ISBN 978-93-83579-62-4

I

First Publication: January 2014

Copyright: Author
            (c) *RAJESHKUMAR A. SHRIMALI*

ISBN 978-93-83579-62-4

Price: Rs.100/-

Published by: Green Flag Foundation
              Sabarkantha, Gujrat-383210, India

.........\ CONTENT /..........

PART 1 : ORGANIZATION MANAGEMENT

PART 2 : CHANGE MANAGEMENT

- Meaning and Important Concepts
- Kinds of Change and the Barriers to Change
- Overcoming Barriers to Change
- The Role of Senior Managers as Barriers to Change
- Global Financial Crisis and Organizational Change
- Why Some Organizations are Better at Driving Change ?
- Role of Catalysts in Organizational Change
- Top-Down versus Bottom-Up Change
- Role of HR in Change Management
- Role of Innovation in Change Management
- Why Change Management Programs Often Fail ? Some Ways to Actualize Change
- Middle Level Management - Sandwich Layer and its Importance to Organizations
- Bureaucracy and Organizational Change
- Change is the only Constant in the 21st Century
- What is Strategic Change ? - Meaning and its Theories
- Change Management: Why the First 100 Days Targets are a Myth ?
- Consequences of the Paradigm Shift
- Organizations of the Future

VI

: PART 1 :
ORGANIZATION MANAGEMENT

- **Organization Management - Meaning, Need and its Features**

A set-up where individuals from diverse backgrounds, different educational qualifications and varied interests come together to work towards a common goal is called an organization.

The employees must work in close coordination with each other and try their level best to achieve the organization's goals.

It is essential to manage the employees well for them to feel indispensable for the organization.

Organization management helps to extract the best out of each employee so that they accomplish the tasks within the given time frame.

Organization management binds the employees together and gives them a sense of loyalty towards the organization.

What is Organization Management ?

Organization management refers to the art of getting people together on a common platform to make them work towards a common predefined goal.

Organization management enables the optimum use of resources through meticulous planning and control at the workplace.

Organization management gives a sense of direction to the employees. The individuals are well aware of their roles and responsibilities and know what they are supposed to do in the organization.

An effective management ensures profitability for the organization. In a layman's language organization management refers to efficient handling of the organization as well as its employees.

Need for Organization Management

- ✓ Organization management gives a sense of security and oneness to the employees.
- ✓ An effective management is required for better coordination among various departments.

✓ Employees accomplish tasks within the stipulated time frame as a result of effective organization management.
✓ Employees stay loyal towards their job and do not treat work as a burden.
✓ Effective organization management leads to a peaceful and positive ambience at the workplace.

Essential Features of Organization Management

1.   Planning

Prepare an effective business plan. It is essential to decide on the future course of action to avoid confusions later on.

Plan out how you intend to do things.

2.   Organizing

Organizing refers to the judicious use of resources to achieve the best out of the employees.

Prepare a monthly budget for smooth cash flow.

3.   Staffing

Poor organization management leads to unhappy employees who eventually create problems for themselves as well as the organization.

Recruit the right talent for the organization.

4.   Leading

The managers or superiors must set clear targets for the team members.

A leader must make sure his team members work in unison towards a common objective. He is the one who decides what would be right in a particular situation.

5.   Control

The superiors must be aware of what is happening around them.

Hierarchies should be well defined for an effective management.

The reporting bosses must review the performance and progress of their subordinates and guide them whenever required.

6.   Time Management

An effective time management helps the employees to do the right thing at the right time.

Managing time effectively always pays in the long run.

7.   Motivation

Motivation goes a long way in binding the employees together.

Appreciating the employees for their good work or lucrative incentive schemes go a long way in motivating the employees and make them work for a longer span of time.

Management Style - Meaning and Different Types of Styles

The art of getting employees together on a common platform and extracting the best out of them refers to effective organization management.

Management plays an important role in strengthening the bond amongst the employees and making them work together as a single unit. It is the management's responsibility to ensure that employees are satisfied with their job responsibilities and eventually deliver their level best.

The management must understand its employees well and strive hard to fulfill their expectations for a stress free ambience at the workplace.

What is Management Style ?

Every leader has a unique style of handling the employees (Juniors/Team). The various ways of dealing with the subordinates at the workplace is called as management style.

The superiors must decide on the future course of action as per the existing culture and conditions at the workplace. The nature of employees and their mindsets also affect the management style of working.

Different Management Styles

1.   Autocratic Style of Working :
   ✓ In such a style of working, the superiors do not take into consideration the ideas and suggestions of the subordinates.

- ✓ The managers, leaders and superiors have the sole responsibility of taking decisions without bothering much about the subordinates.
- ✓ The employees are totally dependent on their bosses and do not have the liberty to take decisions on their own.
- ✓ The subordinates in such a style of working simply adhere to the guidelines and policies formulated by their bosses. They do not have a say in management's decisions.
- ✓ Whatever the superiors feel is right for the organization eventually becomes the company's policies.

Employees lack motivation in autocratic style of working.

2.   Paternalistic Style of Working
- ✓ In paternalistic style of working, the leaders decide what is best for the employees as well as the organization.
- ✓ Policies are devised to benefit the employees and the organization.
- ✓ The suggestions and feedback of the subordinates are taken into consideration before deciding something.
- ✓ In such a style of working, employees feel attached and loyal towards their organization.
- ✓ Employees stay motivated and enjoy their work rather than treating it as a burden.

3.   Democratic Style of Working

In such a style of working, superiors welcome the feedback of the subordinates.
- ✓ Employees are invited on an open forum to discuss the pros and cons of plans and ideas.
- ✓ Democratic style of working ensures effective and healthy communication between the management and the employees.
- ✓ The superiors listen to what the employees have to say before finalizing on something.

4.   Laissez-Faire Style of Working
- ✓ In such a style of working, managers are employed just for the sake of it and do not contribute much to the organization.

✓ The employees take decisions and manage work on their own.
✓ Individuals who have the dream of making it big in the organization and desire to do something innovative every time outshine others who attend office for fun.
✓ Employees are not dependent on the managers and know what is right or wrong for them.

5. Management by Walking Around Style of Working
✓ In the above style of working, managers treat themselves as an essential part of the team and are efficient listeners.
✓ The superiors interact with the employees more often to find out their concerns and suggestions.
✓ In such a style of working, the leader is more of a mentor to its employees and guides them whenever needed.
✓ The managers don't lock themselves in cabins; instead walk around to find out what is happening around them.
✓ Management Skills - Leadership Skills for Efficient Functioning of an Organization

The success and failure of an organization is directly proportional to the effectiveness of the management.

The superiors must share a healthy relationship with the employees for them to deliver their level best.

Leaders need to acquire certain skill sets for an efficient functioning:

Management needs to be impartial towards its employees. Rules and policies should be same for everyone. Favouritism is a strict no no at the workplace. No employee should be granted special favours.

The leaders must promote healthy discussions at the workplace. Make the employees work in teams for them to know each other well. Encourage morning meetings or weekly meetings for the employees to come up with their problems. Issues should not be left unattended. Try not to meet employees separately in closed cabins. Discussions on a common platform are more fruitful and generate better results. Meet the employees once in a week or month as per your schedule. Don't make the meetings too formal. Allow the employees to bring their cups of coffee as well. Individuals do not open up much in formal discussions.

The superiors must ensure that employees do not fight amongst themselves. Conflicts must be avoided at the workplace as nothing productive can be gained out of it. Make sure individuals do not have problems with each other and gel well. In cases of conflicts, management must intervene and sort out differences immediately. Make the employees sit face to face and let them discuss things amongst themselves.

Make sure employees adhere to the rules and regulations of the organization. Set clear objectives for the employees. Targets must be predefined and the employees must know what they are supposed to do at the workplace. Discipline must be maintained at the workplace. The employees must come to work on time and strict action must be taken against those who do not follow company's policies.

Be a good listener. The management must interact with the employees more often. Such initiatives go a long way in motivating the employees and make them stick to the organization for a longer span of time.

The "Hitler approach" does not work in the current scenario. Be a mentor to your employees rather than being a strict boss. Guide them in their work. Try to help them in their assignments. Help them come out with innovative solutions.

Motivate the employees from time to time. Design lucrative incentive plans and schemes to bring out the best in them. Appreciate each time they do good work.

Encourage subordinates to celebrate birthday parties and important festivals at the workplace. Let the employees enjoy together. The seniors must also participate in such activities.

Review the performance of the employees on a regular basis. Make sure employees are satisfied with their job responsibilities. The duties assigned to them must be as per their interests and specialization. Employees not performing up to the mark must be dealt with patience.

The leaders must promote necessary training programmes to upgrade the skills of the existing employees. Team building activities also strengthen the bond amongst the employees.

Make sure employees achieve their targets and organizations earn their profits. Salaries must be distributed on time. The employees must be happy with their job.

Encourage effective communication at the workplace. Communicate more through emails.

Management by Objectives - Meaning, Need and its Limitations

An effective management goes a long way in extracting the best out of employees and make them work as a single unit towards a common goal.

The term Management by Objectives was coined by Peter Drucker in 1954.

What is Management by Objective ?

The process of setting objectives in the organization to give a sense of direction to the employees is called as Management by Objectives.

It refers to the process of setting goals for the employees so that they know what they are supposed to do at the workplace.

Management by Objectives defines roles and responsibilities for the employees and help them chalk out their future course of action in the organization.

Management by objectives guides the employees to deliver their level best and achieve the targets within the stipulated time frame.

Need for Management by Objectives (MBO)

✓ The Management by Objectives process helps the employees to understand their duties at the workplace.
✓ KRAs are designed for each employee as per their interest, specialization and educational qualification.
✓ The employees are clear as to what is expected out of them.

✓ Management by Objectives process leads to satisfied employees. It avoids job mismatch and unnecessary confusions later on.

✓ Employees in their own way contribute to the achievement of the goals and objectives of the organization. Every employee has his own role at the workplace. Each one feels indispensable for the organization and eventually develops a feeling of loyalty towards the organization. They tend to stick to the organization for a longer span of time and contribute effectively. They enjoy at the workplace and do not treat work as a burden.

✓ Management by Objectives ensures effective communication amongst the employees. It leads to a positive ambience at the workplace.

✓ Management by Objectives leads to well defined hierarchies at the workplace. It ensures transparency at all levels. A supervisor of any organization would never directly interact with the Managing Director in case of queries. He would first meet his reporting boss who would then pass on the message to his senior and so on. Every one is clear about his position in the organization.

✓ The MBO Process leads to highly motivated and committed employees.

✓ The MBO Process sets a benchmark for every employee. The superiors set targets for each of the team members. Each employee is given a list of specific tasks.

Limitations of Management by objectives Process

It sometimes ignores the prevailing culture and working conditions of the organization.

▪ More emphasis is being laid on targets and objectives. It just expects the employees to achieve their targets and meet the objectives of the organization without bothering much about the existing circumstances at the workplace. Employees are just expected to perform and meet the deadlines. The MBO Process sometimes do treat individuals as mere machines.

- The MBO process increases comparisons between individuals at the workplace. Employees tend to depend on nasty politics and other unproductive tasks to outshine their fellow workers. Employees do only what their superiors ask them to do. Their work lacks innovation, creativity and sometimes also becomes monotonous.

- **Leadership and Control :**

A set up where individuals from different backgrounds, educational qualifications and varied interests come together on a common platform to achieve certain objectives is called an organization.

What is leadership ?

The art of managing the employees and extracting the best out of them refers to leadership. Employees should not treat their work as a burden for them to deliver their level best at the workplace.

An effective leadership enables the employees to work together as a single unit towards a common goal.

Why leadership at the workplace ?

It is rightly said that success and failure of an organization depends on its leader.

- ✓ Leadership encourages the employees to contribute effectively to the success of their teams as well as the organization.
- ✓ An effective leadership helps the employees to work together in close coordination at the workplace and strive hard to accomplish tasks within the stipulated time frame.
- ✓ A job mismatch at the workplace leads to politics and eventually demotivated employees.
- ✓ A good leader does not impose work on the employees. The roles and responsibilities must be delegated as per the interest and specialization of the individuals.
- ✓ Leadership gives a sense of direction to its employees. Every individual knows what he is supposed to do at the workplace.
- ✓ An effective leadership reduces the chances of politics and conflicts in the organization. Employees stick to an organization for a longer duration under the guidance of able leaders.

- ✓ Employees need someone to guide and correct them whenever they are wrong. A good leader is one who helps the individuals in their assignments and motivates them to deliver results every time.
- ✓ Effective Leadership goes a long way in strengthening the bond amongst the employees and makes them face even the toughest times with a smile.
- ✓ In the current scenario, leaders should be more like mentors rather than being a strict boss. The "Hitler Approach" does not work in the existing situation.
- ✓ It is essential for the leader to interact with the employees more often. Find out what they expect from you as well as the organization. Take initiatives and help them think out of the box.
- ✓ A leader must act as a constant pillar of support for the employees. Individuals must be able to fall back upon the leader at difficult times. Never make fun of their problems or criticize them unnecessarily. Issues must not be left unaddressed.
- ✓ In cases of conflicts, a leader must intervene and sort out the differences immediately. Let individuals sit face to face and discuss their problems amongst themselves. Avoid being partial towards anyone.
- ✓ A leader should be a good role model for the employees. Be a source of inspiration for them.
- ✓ Know what your team members are up to. Keep a track of their work. Performance reviews are essential. Ask the employees to keep you in the loop as well. Appreciate if any of the team members has done well. Individuals not performing up to the mark must be dealt with patience and care.
- ✓ Don't be too harsh on the employees. Understand their problems as well. Don't expect an individual to attend office on his birthday or anniversary. Be a little more realistic.

To conclude leadership encourages the employees to trust their mentors and count on them always at the workplace.

- **What is Organization Development ?**

A set up which brings together individuals from different backgrounds, varied interests and specializations on a common platform for them to work as a single unit and achieve certain predefined goals is called an organization.

An organization must make money for its survival. It is essential for the employees to deliver their level best and eventually increase the productivity of the organization.

- **What is Organization Development ?**

Organization Development refers to the various ways and procedures to increase the productivity and effectiveness of an organization.

Organization Development includes the various techniques which help the employees as well as the organization adjust to changing circumstances in a better way.

- **Why Organization Development ?**

The concept of Organization development enables the organization to achieve the targets and meet the objectives at a much faster rate.

✓ The employees as a result of organization development respond better to changes in the work culture.

✓ Organization development helps the employees to focus on their jobs and contribute in their best possible way.

✓ Management can handle the employees in a better way as a result of organization development.

Kurt Lewin is ideally believed to be the father of Organization development.

- **When is the Organization Ready for Development ?**

1. First Step - Dissatisfied with the current scenario: The employees are not happy with the current scenario and feel the need for a change in the processes of the organization.

2. Second Step - Suggesting Changes: In the second step, employees discuss amongst themselves the various options which would help the organization do better in the near future.

3. Third Step - Applying the processes: Various policies and procedures are applied to help the organization respond to external as well as internal changes more effectively.

- **Understanding Organization**

A six step model for understanding organization was proposed by Weisbord The goals and objectives of the organization must be clearly defined. The employees must be aware of their duties and functions in the organization. The individuals must know what is expected out of them at the workplace.

- ✓ It is essential to divide the work amongst the individuals as per their interests, specialization, experience and educational qualification. Job mismatch should be avoided as it leads to demotivated employees. Let the individuals decide what best they can do.

- ✓ The employees must share a cordial relationship with each other. Conflicts and unnecessary misunderstandings lead to a negative ambience at the workplace. There should be coordination between various departments for better results. Transparency is a must at all levels. Individuals must discuss matters among themselves before reaching to final conclusions. The departments must support each other in their work.

- ✓ It is important to appreciate the ones who perform well. Those who do well must be admired in front of all to motivate them and expect the same from them every time. The management must make the non performers realize their mistakes and ask them to pull up their socks. They should not be criticized, instead dealt with patience and care. Give them opportunities but still if they don't perform up to the mark, punish them.

- ✓ Leaders should be more like mentors and must provide a sense of direction to the employees. They should bind the employees together and extract the best out of them. The superiors must be a source of inspiration for the subordinates.

- ✓ Promote training programs to upgrade the skills of employees and help them face the challenges and changes in the organization with utmost determination. Plan your resources well.

- **Communication at Workplace**
  - ✓ Communication plays an important role in the success and failure of an organization. The art of expressing one's ideas and thoughts clearly is called as effective communication. Individuals need to communicate effectively at the workplace for better transparency and clarity. Not only effective communication helps in correct transfer of information but also in decision making.
  - ✓ Be very clear as to what you expect form your fellow workers. Mention all the details and do cross check whether the other person has noted it correctly or not. Do not expect the other person to understand everything on his own. Don't blame him afterwards.
  - ✓ Avoid using derogatory sentences or foul words against anyone at the workplace. One should maintain the decorum of the organization. It is better to avoid people rather than fighting with them.
  - ✓ Employees should depend more on written modes of communication. Communicate through Emails as records are available even later on. The mails must be marked to all the related individuals with a cc to the superiors for them to know what is happening around. Make sure the mails are self explanatory. Don't write colourful and casual mails.
  - ✓ Develop the habit of using planners, notepads and organizers. It is practically not possible for an individual to remember everything. One must note down important tasks against deadlines to avoid forgetting things. Be organized. Use a desktop calendar and keep it right in front of your eyes.
  - ✓ Never play with words. Don't try to confuse the other person. Pass on the information in its desired form.
  - ✓ During meetings, seminars and presentations, don't just speak for the front benchers. One must be audible even to the person

sitting on the last row. Neither speak too fast nor too slow. Be confident while you speak. One should be loud and clear. Make sure you are understood by all.

✓ Never use a fake accent at workplace. Be careful where to use the punctuation marks.

✓ Employees must not enter meeting room or board room without pen and a notepad. Jot down your queries at one place and ask only when the other person has finished his speech or presentation.

✓ Do not interfere when others are speaking. Let them first finish their conversation. Wait for your turn to speak.

✓ One should never shout at the workplace. Shouting and conflicts spoil the ambience at the workplace. Handle the issues intelligently and a little diplomatically. Avoid arguing with anyone as it leads to no solution. It always pays to be soft-spoken at workplace.

✓ While interacting over the phone, make sure you spell out the words for better clarity. Use simple words to denote alphabets like t as in tango, a as in alpha and so on. Chances of misunderstandings are very less in such cases.

✓ Don't chew anything while you are speaking over the phone. Avoid laughing or giggling.

✓ Be a patient listener. Listen to what the second party has to say. Don't jump to conclusions.

✓ Be very careful about the content of your speech. Make sure your words do not hurt any of your fellow workers.

- **Work Culture - Meaning, Importance & Characterics of a Healthy Culture**

An organization is formed to achieve certain goals and objectives by bringing individuals together on a common platform and motivating them to deliver their level best. It is essential for the employees to enjoy at the workplace for them to develop a sense of loyalty towards it.

Work culture plays an important role in extracting the best out of employees and making them stick to the organization for a longer duration. The organization must offer a positive ambience to the employees for them to concentrate on their work rather than interfering in each other's work.

What is work culture ?

Work culture is a concept which deals in the study of:

✓ Beliefs, thought processes, attitudes of the employees.

✓ Ideologies and principles of the organization.

It is the work culture which decides the way employees interact with each other and how an organization functions.

In layman's language work culture refers to the mentality of the employees which further decides the ambience of the organization.

An organization is said to have a strong work culture when the employees follow the organization's rules and regulations and adhere to the existing guidelines. However there are certain organizations where employees are reluctant to follow the instructions and are made to work only by strict procedures. Such organizations have a weak culture.

Characteristics of a Healthy work Culture

✓ A healthy work culture leads to satisfied employees and an increased productivity.

✓ Employees must be cordial with each other. One must respect his fellow worker. Backbiting is considered strictly unprofessional and must be avoided for a healthy work culture. One gains nothing out of conflicts and nasty politics at work.

✓ Each employee should be treated as one. Partiality leads to demotivated employees and eventually an unhealthy work culture. Employees should be judged only by their work and nothing else. Personal relationships should take a backseat at the workplace. Don't favour anyone just because he is your relative.

✓ Appreciating the top performers is important. Praise the employees to expect good work from them every time. Give them a pat on their back. Let them feel indispensable for their organization. Don't criticize the ones who have not performed well, instead ask them to pull up their socks for the next time. Give them one more opportunity rather than firing them immediately.

✓ Encourage discussions at the workplace. Employees must discuss issues among themselves to reach to better conclusions. Each one should have the liberty to express his views. The team leaders and managers must interact with the subordinates frequently. Transparency is essential at all levels for better relationships among employees and a healthy work culture. Manipulating information and data tampering is a strict no no at the workplace. Let information flow in its desired form.

✓ Organization must have employee friendly policies and practical guidelines. Expecting an employee to work till late night on his birthday is simply impractical. Rules and regulations should be made to benefit the employees. Employees must maintain the decorum of the organization. Discipline is important at the workplace.

✓ The "Hitler approach" does not fit in the current scenario. Bosses should be more like mentors to the employees. The team leaders should be a source of inspiration for the subordinates. The superiors are expected to provide a sense of direction to the employees and guide them whenever needed. The team members should have an easy access to their boss's cabin.

✓ Promote team building activities to bind the employees together. Conduct training programs, workshops, seminars and presentations to upgrade the existing skills of the employees. Prepare them for the tough times. They should be ready under any odd circumstances or change in the work culture.

- **Organization Ethics - Meaning and its Importance**

An organization is formed when individuals from different backgrounds and varied interests come together on a common platform and work towards predefined goals and objectives.

Employees are the assets of an organization and it is essential for them to maintain the decorum and ambience of the workplace.

What is organization Ethics ?

The way an organization should respond to external environment refers to organization ethics. Organization ethics includes various guidelines and principles which decide the way individuals should behave at the workplace.

It also refers to the code of conduct of the individuals working in a particular organization.

Every organization runs to earn profits but how it makes money is more important. No organization should depend on unfair means to earn money. One must understand that money is not the only important thing; pride and honour are more important. An individual's first priority can be to make money but he should not stoop too low just to be able to do that.

Children below fourteen years of age must not be employed to work in any organization. Childhood is the best phase of one's life and no child should be deprived of his childhood.

Employees should not indulge in destruction or manipulation of information to get results. Data Tampering is considered strictly unethical and unprofessional in the corporate world. Remember if one is honest, things will always be in his favour.

Employees should not pass on company's information to any of the external parties. Do not share any of your organization's policies and guidelines with others. It is better not to discuss official matters with friends and relatives. Confidential data or information must not be leaked under any circumstances.

There must be absolute fairness in monetary transactions and all kinds of trading. Never ever cheat your clients.

Organizations must not discriminate any employee on the grounds of sex, physical appearance, age or family background. Female employees must be treated with respect. Don't ask your female employees to stay back late at work. It is unethical to discriminate employees just because they do not belong to an affluent background. Employees should be judged by their work and nothing else.

Organization must not exploit any of the employees. The employees must be paid according to their hard work and efforts. If individuals are working late at night, make sure overtimes are paid. The management must ensure employees get their arrears, bonus, incentives and other reimbursements on time.

Stealing office property is strictly unethical.

Organization must take care of the safety of the employees. Individuals should not be exposed to hazardous conditions.

Never lie to your customers. It is unprofessional to make false promises to the consumers. The advertisements must give a clear picture of the product. Do not commit anything which your organization can't offer. It is important to be honest with your customers to expect loyalty from them. It is absolutely unethical to fool the customers.

The products should not pose a threat to environment and mankind.

Employees on probation period can be terminated anytime but organizations need to give one month notice before firing the permanent ones. In the same way permanent employees need to serve one month notice before resigning from the current services. Employees can't stop coming to office all of a sudden.

- **Common Threats to an Organization**

What do you understand by threats to an organization? Threats refer to negative influences which not only hamper the productivity of an organization but also bring a bad name to it.

Let us go through common threats faced by an organization.

One of the most common threats faced by organization is employees with a negative approach. Remember; nothing can harm an organization more than unfaithful employees. Believe me, employees who attend office just to earn their salaries are in fact the biggest threat to an organization. Non serious employees do not contribute much towards the productivity of an organization. They are a mere burden on the system. Even the best of clients, best of infrastructure or the best of machinery would not help if people associated with the organization are not loyal and committed towards it.

High attrition rate is another big threat to an organization. Organizations suffer a great loss when talented employees quit and join their competitors. When an individual who has been trained for six months by an organization leaves all of a sudden, it is both waste of time and energy. Make sure employees who know their job and responsibilities well stick to the organization for a long time at least for two to three years.

Another common threat faced by an organization is data and information loss. A lot of effort goes in formulating important strategies for the team and organization. It is unethical to share confidential information with your competitors. When individuals have their best friends within the organization but working in separate teams, they tend to share team strategies and policies. In such a case not only respective teams suffer but also the entire organization. Client data base, monetary transactions, company accounts, salaries of employees need to be kept confidential under all circumstances.

In today's business scenario, where individuals are totally dependent on their computers, everything goes for a toss if system crashes. Believe me; a server failure can lead to major losses for the organization. A lot of time goes in first detecting as to what went wrong and then rectifying the problem. Employees find it extremely difficult to deliver if their machines are not in proper working conditions. They can neither fetch any data nor interact with their clients through emails. Instruct employees to take proper backups at regular intervals. IT department is the lifeline of every organization and they need to ensure proper softwares and anti viruses are installed in every machine. Do not keep untrained professionals in your IT team. Another major problem arises when telephone lines are out of order.

Security issues pose a major threat to the organization. Make sure you have appointed security staffs who are responsible for the overall security of the organization as well as safety of the employees.

Proper measures need to be taken to protect the organization from fire, earth quake or any other disaster of similar sort. It becomes organization's primary responsibility to take care of its employees and their basic requirements. Poor working condition does not allow employees to give their hundred percent.

Mass boycotts and strikes also pose major threat to organization. Situations where individuals tend to form groups and go on strikes not only affect the productivity of the organization but also spoil the work culture.

Lack of funds is another area of concern for the organizations. Financial stability is of utmost importance and organizations need to have a stable background. A situation where you are unable to give salaries to your employees and also meet daily expenses need to be avoided at any cost. Planning is essential. An organization needs to have sufficient funds to survive the challenging times.

- **Role of Employees in Reducing Threats to Organization**

Employees are the backbone of every organization. They play a crucial role in controlling and also reducing the threats to organization. The major threat to an organization is a non serious employee who attends office just for the sake of it. Individuals need to love their organization for them to deliver their level best.

The first initiative towards reducing threat to organization is to genuinely develop a feeling of respect for your organization. Do not love your organization just because your Boss has asked you to do so. The feeling needs to come from within. The moment you are loyal towards your organization, your productivity would increase manifold eventually benefitting the organization. Do not work just for your salary. After all money is not everything. Your career and professional goals are more important.

Keep confidential information to yourself. You can have best friends at the workplace but you really do not have to discuss work and team strategies with him /her. There are other things to discuss as well. Do not pass on information to your competitors. Trust me; it is in fact a crime to do so. If caught, not only would it spoil your entire career but also bring a bad name to you and your family. A sense of commitment towards the organization is essential. It is unacceptable on part of a mature professional to share data, figures, balance sheets, salaries of employees, business strategies with not only competitors but also clients as well as friends within the organization. Data hacking is one of the cheapest activities an employee can indulge into.

Take care of your office property. Make sure your office machine is used only for official purposes and not for downloading movies, uploading personal pictures and so on. Use your office computer the same way you use your personal laptop. Make sure the computer is switched off properly. Do not simply turn off the main button. It will crash your system. Your official email id should be strictly used for official purposes only and nothing else. Do not chat with your friends and relatives from your official email account.

Do not indulge in nasty office politics. Remember, going on strikes is not the only solution. Rather than indulging in unproductive activities, damaging office property, influencing co workers not to work, it is always better to sit face to face, discuss, sort out issues and reach to mutually beneficial solutions. Do not play blame games at workplace. Never spoil the work culture. Make your organization a happy place to work.

Respect organization policies. Keep important documents and files at proper places and make sure you lock your drawers properly before you leave for the day. Also lock your cabin properly so that no one else can enter and steal important data once you are out of the office. If you do not adhere to the security policies of your organization, do not be surprised if your competitor comes out with marketing strategies which you have formulated a month ago with your team mates. Lock your systems carefully. Do not keep common passwords which others can predict easily. Keep your workstations tidy and never write important pass words, account details on loose papers. All important documents need to be put in the paper shredder first before finally disposing. You never know when someone can misuse the information written on them.

Memorize routes to safe areas from your work station in case of fire. Do know where the fire extinguisher is kept and also how to operate the same. An employee needs to know all emergency exits and also acquaint themselves with emergency evacuation procedures. Be prepared to face unwanted situations and remember never to panic.

Role of HR Consulting in Redesigning Organizational Structure

Organizational structure is the driving force behind the performance and growth of the organization. For an organization to achieve success and competitive advantage, it is highly important that there should be complete alignment between the organizational structure and the strategic goals of the organization. A properly coordinated organizational structure improves the flow of information and communication within the organisation.

Generally, changes in different aspects like political, cultural, competitive, market, technologies, business requirements, resources, regulations, business goals, organic growth, leadership changes, mergers and acquisitions, etc. may trigger the need to redesign the structure of the organization. The organization's structure should fit properly with the changing needs and objectives of the organization, and the market conditions as well, to maintain its efficiency in the long run.

An obsolete organizational structure results in:
- ✓ Inefficient organization
- ✓ Lack of both, inter as well as intra units/ departmental, coordination
- ✓ Ambiguous role definition
- ✓ Emergence of conflicts in the workplace
- ✓ Disrupted or elongated flow of work and processes
- ✓ Multiple superior/ supervisor issues
- ✓ Creation of various extra organizational committees, departments, and units
- ✓ Improper utilization of resources
- ✓ Employee dissatisfaction
- ✓ High turnover rates

Therefore, for an organization it is very important to revise and update its structure to maintain its purpose and functionality. Further, redesigning organizational structure helps in improving internal processes and employee engagement, thereby, favourably affecting the financial performance and competitive position of the organization.

Organisational structure redesigning involves alignment of the organizational structure to the business strategies by providing appropriately redesigned model for the existing structure, implementing the new structure, and necessary strategies for downsizing or related changes in the structure.

An HR Consulting Firm can diligently perform the task of analyzing and redesigning the structure of the organisation in accordance with the strategic goals, objectives and mission of the organization.

While performing the task of organizational structuring, HR Consultants should consider following issues:

- ✓ The purpose, objectives, goals and strategies of the organization or the specific units
- ✓ The navigation of work flow and processes to be simplified and standardised
- ✓ The needs, requirements and expectations of the clients are met with
- ✓ Maintaining effective flow of communication within the organization
- ✓ Enough room for employment development and career progression for the employees
- ✓ Efficient as well as effective utilization of the resources available for the organization
- ✓ Complying with the legal formalities
- ✓ Creating a structure which creates a motivating and satisfying environment for the employees
- ✓ Understanding the market trends and industry norms/ best practices

- ✓ The process of organizational structuring involves following comprehensive stages:
- ✓ Assessment of the organization's structure, as it exists in the current situation and as it had existed before any of the previous changes or revisions.
- ✓ Identification of the root causes of organizational performance related issues.
- ✓ The analysis is them examined in relation to the organizational culture, strategic goals and business objectives. Again, both the existing factors as well as previous factors are considered here. Future, future strategic goals and objectives are also taken into consideration so that the revised organizational structure caters to the current as well as the future needs of the organization.
- ✓ Preparation of the revised or updated organizational structure.
- ✓ Implementation of the structural changes keeping in mind that the implementation should bring in least distraction to the organizations operation.
- ✓ An evaluation is then carried out regarding the efficiency and fluency brought in by the changed organizational structure.

Thus, HR Consultants can facilitate in the development and designing of an effective organizational structure which optimizes the resource utilization and promotes growth of the organization.

- ▪ **Understanding Organization and Organization Culture**
  What is an organization ?

An organization is nothing but a common platform where individuals from different backgrounds come together and work as a collective unit to achieve certain objectives and targets. The word organization derived from the Greek work "organon" is a set up where people join hands to earn a living for themselves as well as earn profits for the company. An organization consists of individuals with different specializations, educational qualifications and work experiences all working towards a common goal. Here the people are termed as employees.

The employees are the major assets of an organization and contribute effectively in its successful functioning. It is essential for the employees to be loyal towards their organization and strive hard in furthering its brand image. An organization can't survive if the employees are not at all serious about it and treat their work as a burden. The employees must enjoy whatever they do for them to deliver their level best.

What is culture ?

The attitude, traits and behavioral patterns which govern the way an individual interacts with others is termed as culture. Culture is something which one inherits from his ancestors and it helps in distinguishing one individual from the other.

What is organization culture ?

Every human being has certain personality traits which help them stand apart from the crowd. No two individuals behave in a similar way. In the same way organizations have certain values, policies, rules and guidelines which help them create an image of their own.

Organization culture refers to the beliefs and principles of a particular organization. The culture followed by the organization has a deep impact on the employees and their relationship amongst themselves.

Every organization has a unique culture making it different from the other and giving it a sense of direction. It is essential for the employees to understand the culture of their workplace to adjust well.

Organization A

In organization A, the employees are not at all disciplined and are least bothered about the rules and regulations. They reach their office at their own sweet time and spend their maximum time gossiping and loitering around.

Organization B

This organization follows employee friendly policies and it is mandatory for all to adhere to them. It is important for the employees to reach their workplace on time and no one is allowed to unnecessarily roam around or spread rumours.

Which organization do you feel would perform better ? — Obviously organization B

The employees follow a certain culture in organization B making it more successful than organization A.

No two organizations can have the same culture. The values or policies of a non-profit organization would be different from that of a profit making entity or employees working in a restaurant would follow a different culture as compared to those associated with education industry or a manufacturing industry.

Broadly there are two types of organization culture:

- ✓ Strong Organization Culture: Strong organizational culture refers to a situation where the employees adjust well, respect the organization's policies and adhere to the guidelines. In such a culture people enjoy working and take every assignment as a new learning and try to gain as much as they can. They accept their roles and responsibilities willingly.

- ✓ Weak Organization Culture: In such a culture individuals accept their responsibilities out of fear of superiors and harsh policies. The employees in such a situation do things out of compulsion. They just treat their organization as a mere source of earning money and never get attached to it.

Types of Organization Culture

The practices, principles, policies and values of an organization form its culture. The culture of an organization decides the way employees behave amongst themselves as well as the people outside the organization.

Let us understand the various types of organization culture:

1.	Normative Culture: In such a culture, the norms and procedures of the organization are predefined and the rules and regulations are set as per the existing guidelines. The employees behave in an ideal way and strictly adhere to the policies of the organization. No employee dares to break the rules and sticks to the already laid policies.

2.   Pragmatic Culture: In a pragmatic culture, more emphasis is placed on the clients and the external parties. Customer satisfaction is the main motive of the employees in a pragmatic culture. Such organizations treat their clients as Gods and do not follow any set rules. Every employee strives hard to satisfy his clients to expect maximum business from their side.

3.   Academy Culture: Organizations following academy culture hire skilled individuals. The roles and responsibilities are delegated according to the back ground, educational qualification and work experience of the employees. Organizations following academy culture are very particular about training the existing employees. They ensure that various training programmes are being conducted at the workplace to hone the skills of the employees. The management makes sincere efforts to upgrade the knowledge of the employees to improve their professional competence. The employees in an academy culture stick to the organization for a longer duration and also grow within it. Educational institutions, universities, hospitals practice such a culture.

4.   Baseball team Culture: A baseball team culture considers the employees as the most treasured possession of the organization. The employees are the true assets of the organization who have a major role in its successful functioning. In such a culture, the individuals always have an upper edge and they do not bother much about their organization. Advertising agencies, event management companies, financial institutions follow such a culture.

5.   Club Culture: Organizations following a club culture are very particular about the employees they recruit. The individuals are hired as per their specialization, educational qualification and interests. Each one does what he is best at. The high potential employees are promoted suitably and appraisals are a regular feature of such a culture.

6.   Fortress Culture: There are certain organizations where the employees are not very sure about their career and longevity. Such organizations follow fortress culture. The employees are terminated if the organization is not performing well. Individuals suffer the most

when the organization is at a loss. Stock broking industries follow such a culture.

7.   Tough Guy Culture: In a tough guy culture, feedbacks are essential. The performance of the employees is reviewed from time to time and their work is thoroughly monitored. Team managers are appointed to discuss queries with the team members and guide them whenever required. The employees are under constant watch in such a culture.

8.   Bet your company Culture: Organizations which follow bet your company culture take decisions which involve a huge amount of risk and the consequences are also unforeseen. The principles and policies of such an organization are formulated to address sensitive issues and it takes time to get the results.

9.   Process Culture: As the name suggests the employees in such a culture adhere to the processes and procedures of the organization. Feedbacks and performance reviews do not matter much in such organizations. The employees abide by the rules and regulations and work according to the ideologies of the workplace. All government organizations follow such a culture.

- **Importance of Organization Culture**

A common platform where individuals work in unison to earn profits as well as a livelihood for themselves is called an organization. A place where individuals realize the dream of making it big is called an organization. Every organization has its unique style of working which often contributes to its culture. The beliefs, ideologies, principles and values of an organization form its culture. The culture of the workplace controls the way employees behave amongst themselves as well as with people outside the organization.

- ✓ The culture decides the way employees interact at their workplace. A healthy culture encourages the employees to stay motivated and loyal towards the management.
- ✓ The culture of the workplace also goes a long way in promoting healthy competition at the workplace. Employees try their level best to perform better than their fellow workers and earn

recognition and appreciation of the superiors. It is the culture of the workplace which actually motivates the employees to perform.

✓ Every organization must have set guidelines for the employees to work accordingly. The culture of an organization represents certain predefined policies which guide the employees and give them a sense of direction at the workplace. Every individual is clear about his roles and responsibilities in the organization and know how to accomplish the tasks ahead of the deadlines.

✓ No two organizations can have the same work culture. It is the culture of an organization which makes it distinct from others. The work culture goes a long way in creating the brand image of the organization. The work culture gives an identity to the organization. In other words, an organization is known by its culture.

✓ The organization culture brings all the employees on a common platform. The employees must be treated equally and no one should feel neglected or left out at the workplace. It is essential for the employees to adjust well in the organization culture for them to deliver their level best.

✓ The work culture unites the employees who are otherwise from different back grounds, families and have varied attitudes and mentalities. The culture gives the employees a sense of unity at the workplace.

✓ Certain organizations follow a culture where all the employees irrespective of their designations have to step into the office on time. Such a culture encourages the employees to be punctual which eventually benefits them in the long run. It is the culture of the organization which makes the individuals a successful professional.

✓ Every employee is clear with his roles and responsibilities and strives hard to accomplish the tasks within the desired time frame as per the set guidelines. Implementation of policies is never a problem in organizations where people follow a set culture. The new employees also try their level best to understand the work culture and make the organization a better place to work.

✓ The work culture promotes healthy relationship amongst the employees. No one treats work as a burden and moulds himself according to the culture.

It is the culture of the organization which extracts the best out of each team member. In a culture where management is very particular about the reporting system, the employees however busy they are would send their reports by end of the day. No one has to force anyone to work. The culture develops a habit in the individuals which makes them successful at the workplace.

- **Factors Affecting Organization Culture**

Culture represents the beliefs, ideologies, policies, practices of an organization. It gives the employees a sense of direction and also controls the way they behave with each other. The work culture brings all the employees on a common platform and unites them at the workplace.

There are several factors which affect the organization culture:

The first and the foremost factor affecting culture is the individual working with the organization. The employees in their own way contribute to the culture of the workplace. The attitudes, mentalities, interests, perception and even the thought process of the employees affect the organization culture.

Example - Organizations which hire individuals from army or defence background tend to follow a strict culture where all the employees abide by the set guidelines and policies. The employees are hardly late to work. It is the mindset of the employees which forms the culture of the place. Organizations with majority of youngsters encourage healthy competition at the workplace and employees are always on the toes to perform better than the fellow workers.

The sex of the employee also affects the organization culture. Organizations where male employees dominate the female counterparts follow a culture where late sitting is a normal feature. The male employees are more aggressive than the females who instead would be caring and softhearted.

The nature of the business also affects the culture of the organization. Stock broking industries, financial services, banking industry are all dependent on external factors like demand and supply, market cap, earning per share and so on. When the market crashes, these industries have no other option than to terminate the employees and eventually affect the culture of the place. Market fluctuations lead to unrest, tensions and severely demotivate the individuals. The management also feels helpless when circumstances can be controlled by none. Individuals are unsure about their career as well as growth in such organizations.

The culture of the organization is also affected by its goals and objectives. The strategies and procedures designed to achieve the targets of the organization also contribute to its culture.

Individuals working with government organizations adhere to the set guidelines but do not follow a procedure of feedback thus forming its culture. Fast paced industries like advertising, event management companies expect the employees to be attentive, aggressive and hyper active.

The clients and the external parties to some extent also affect the work culture of the place. Organizations catering to UK and US Clients have no other option but to work in shifts to match their timings, thus forming the culture.

The management and its style of handling the employees also affect the culture of the workplace. There are certain organizations where the management allows the employees to take their own decisions and let them participate in strategy making. In such a culture, employees get attached to their management and look forward to a long term association with the organization. The management must respect the employees to avoid a culture where the employees just work for money and nothing else. They treat the organization as a mere source of earning money and look for a change in a short span of time.

- ### Changing Organizational Culture

A common set up where individuals from different back grounds, educational qualifications, interests and perception come together and use their skills to earn revenue is called an organization. The successful functioning of an organization depends on the effort put by each employee. Each individual has to contribute his level best to accomplish the tasks within the desired time frame.

Every organization has a unique style of working which is often called its culture. The beliefs, policies, principles, ideologies of an organization form its culture.

The culture of the organization is nothing but the outcome of the interaction among the employees working for quite some time. The behaviour of the individual with his fellow workers as well as external parties forms the culture. The management style of dealing with the employees in its own way also contributes to the culture of the organization.

Employees working for a considerable amount of time in any particular organization tend to make certain rules and follow some policies as per their convenience and mutual understanding. Such policies and procedures practised by the employees for a long time to make the workplace a happier place form the culture. The culture often gives the employees a sense of direction at the workplace.

Organization culture however can never be constant. It changes with time.

Let us understand the concept with the help of an example.

Organization A was a well-known event management firm. Tom, Sandra, Peter and Jack represented the management. All the four were in their mid-thirties and thus emphasized on hiring young talent. No wonders this organization followed a youth culture. The employees were aggressive, on their toes and eager to do something innovative always. The organization followed a macho culture where the employees performing exceptionally well were appreciated and rewarded suitably. Appraisals and promotions came in no time and feedbacks were quick. The management also encouraged in formal get-togethers, dinners to bring the employees closer and increase the comfort level.

After proving their mettle for quite some years, Tom, Sandra and Peter decided to move on for better opportunities. Tim, Maria, Sara all in their fifties stepped into their shoes and took the charge along with Jack, the only member left from the previous team. They did not somehow approve the previous style of working. They brought their own people from their previous organizations and thus caused problems for the existing employees. The management strongly supported punctuality and did not quite promote parties; get-togethers at workplace. There were no feedbacks or rewards. The employees lacked enthusiasm and never bothered to do something innovative.

Is there any change in the work culture ?

A change in the management changed the entire style of working.

- **Reasons for changes in work culture**
  - ✓ A new management, a new team leader, a new boss brings a change in the organization culture. A new employee but obvious would have new ideas, concepts and try his level best to implement them. He would want the employees to work according to him. His style of working, behaviour and ideologies would definitely bring a change in the work culture.
  - ✓ Financial loss, bankruptcy, market fluctuations also lead to change in the work culture of the organization. When an organization runs into losses, it fails to give rewards and appraisals to the employees as it used to give earlier.
  - ✓ Acquiring new clients might cause a change in the work culture. The employees might have to bring about a change in their style of working to meet the expectations of the new clients.
  - ✓ The employees on their own might realize that they need to bring a change in their attitude, perception and style of working to achieve the targets at a much faster rate. Such self-realization also changes the work culture.

- **Adjusting to Changing Organization Culture**

The work culture represents the ideologies, principles, policies and beliefs of the organization. The individual's style of working, his behaviour and ways of interaction also contribute to the culture of the organization.

There are several reasons which lead to a change in the organization culture. Change in management, poor financial conditions, revisions in goals and targets bring a change in the culture of the organization.

Accepting changes in the work culture is the toughest thing to do for an employee. Not all employees can happily adapt to organizational changes.

Employees need time to cope up with a new culture. Miracles can't happen overnight and habits do not change all of a sudden. The employees must spend some time to understand and adjust to the new culture. One should work with an open mind and willingly accept things. Don't always crib as it leads to no solution. The employees must try their level best to accept the changes with a smile and work accordingly. One should never be in a rush. The management must also give time to the employees for them to gel with the new culture. Don't pressurize anyone to accept changes all of a sudden.

The employees must design new strategies, new plan of actions and policies to meet the new challenges. Try to find out the exact reasons for the change. The ideas which were successful earlier might now fall out of place. One should not be adamant. Sit with your team leader, discuss all possible options and try to implement something which would work best in the new culture and benefit you as well as your organization.

An employee must change his behaviour and thought process as per the culture. It is essential to be flexible. Being adaptable at the workplace always pays in the long run. Remember everything happens for the best. One should always try to look at the positive aspects of life rather than cribbing on things which are beyond anyone's control.

Janet worked with an organization of repute. Her organization followed a culture where the employees never reached office on time.

There were no strict rules and regulations for the employees. Janet found her work culture very comfortable as there was no pressure on her to reach work on time.

Very soon her organization hired someone from its competitor to take charge of the organization. He made several changes in the work culture, the first and the foremost being fixed timings for all the emloyees.Everyone irrespective of the designation had to reach office on time. All the employees had to adhere to the guidelines and policies of the organization.

Condition A

Janet found it very difficult to adjust to the new culture. She could not accept the sudden change in the work culture, cribbed amongst her fellow workers and found her work as a burden.

Condition B

Janet happily accepted the change and tried her level best to adjust to it.She was intelligent enough to understand that after all the change was for the benefit of the organization. She got up little early everyday and reached office on time. She gave her best everyday and won the appreciation of her superiors as well as the management.

Which situation do you feel is better ?

Obviously Situation B

One should always remember that a little change in one's behaviour can make the organization a better place to work.

Few tips to adjust to the changing organization culture.

  i.   Give time to adjust
 ii.   Be flexible
iii.   Work with an open mind
 iv.   Never crib
  v.   Look at the positive side
 vi.   Develop alternate plans
vii.   Don't get too attached to someone at the workplace

Role of Employees in Organization Culture

A place where individuals from different backgrounds, religions, communities come together on a common platform to work towards a predefined goal is called an organization. Every organization has set of principles and policies mandatory for all the employees to follow.

The beliefs, ideologies and practices of an organization form its culture which gives a sense of direction to the employees. The work culture goes a long way in creating the brand image of the organization and making it distinct from its competitors. The employees are the true assets of an organization. They are the ones who contribute effectively towards the successful functioning of an organization. They strive hard to deliver their level best and achieve the assigned targets within the stipulated time frame.

The employees play an important role in deciding the culture of the workplace. Their behaviour, attitude and interest at the workplace form the culture.

Let us understand how employees affect the work culture.

Please go through the below cases:

Organization A

The employees are least bothered about the policies of the organization and attend work just to sustain their job. For them the workplace is nothing but a mere source of earning money. In such a scenario, people seldom get attached to their organization and thus move on in a very short span of time.

Organization B

In organization B, employees are particular about the rules and regulations of the organization and adhere to the set guidelines. The individuals focus on their work and look forward to achieving it well ahead of the deadlines. People stay away from unnecessary gossips and prefer sitting at their workstations rather than loitering around.

Organization C

Organization C is a male oriented organization where male employees dominate their female counterparts. Frequent late sitting is a regular feature of the organization culture. Employees prefer staying back late to finish off their pending work. No organization expects its employees to stay back; it is the employee who according to his own convenience adjusts the timings and makes it the culture of the workplace.

In all the above situations it is the style of working and the behaviour of the employees which form the culture of the workplace. The thought processes and assumptions of the members of the organization contribute to its culture. A motivated and a satisfied employee would promote a healthy culture at the workplace as compared to a demotivated employee.

There are certain organizations where the employees willingly accept challenges and learn something new each day. The roles and responsibilities are delegated as per the interest and specialization of the employees and thus each one tries hard to perform better than the fellow workers. Such organizations follow a strong culture as employees are serious about their work and abide by the policies. However there are certain organizations where things need to be imposed on the employees. They somehow have to be forced by the management to perform their duties. Team leaders have to be appointed to monitor their performance and make them work. In such cases organization follow a weak culture.

Some organizations have aggressive employees who promote healthy competition at the workplace. Such organizations follow a culture where every individual tries hard to win the appreciation of the management. Recognition hungry employees encourage a positive culture at the workplace as compared to organizations where people have nothing innovative to do.

Constant disputes, disagreements, leg pulling lead to a negative ambience at the workplace. Employees find it difficult to concentrate in such a culture and look for a change.

Role of Communication and Relationship for a Healthy Organization Culture

The ideologies, principles, rules and policies of an organization form its culture. The ways the employees interact amongst themselves and with others outside the organization contribute to the culture of the workplace. The culture gives an identity to the organization and makes it distinct from others.

Communication and relationship play an important role in a healthy organization culture.

Effective communication is essential for a positive culture at the workplace. Transparency in communication is mandatory at all levels for better understanding of work and better bonding among individuals.

Culture is simply the result of the interaction amongst the employees working for a considerable period of time in the organization. A better employee relation promotes a positive culture whereas conflicts and disagreements spoil the ambience and spread negativity all around at the workplace.

Communication plays an important role in increasing the comfort factor amongst the employees and eventually a healthy culture at the workplace.

The communication between the top management and the employee needs to be effective for better work culture. The management must clearly pass on necessary information to all the employees so that they know what they actually are supposed to do at the workplace. The employees must be very clear with their key responsibility areas for them to deliver their level best. The roles and responsibilities must be delegated as per specialization, educational qualification and area of interest.

The employees should have the liberty to share their ideas and concepts on an open forum to come to an innovative solution benefitting all. It is essential to come to an alternative acceptable to one and all for a healthy culture at the workplace. Discussions are important before implementing any new idea.

The consistent performers must have a say in the strategy making. Such activities go a long way in motivating the employees and creating a culture where employees stick to the organization for a long time.

- ✓ Morning meetings are essential to effectively communicate the agenda of the day to one and all. Every employee should be treated equally and no one should feel neglected or left out at the workplace. Quick feedbacks are important.
- ✓ The employees must develop the habit of using planners and organizers to avoid forgetting critical issues.
- ✓ More emphasis should be laid on written communication as compared to verbal communication as no one can ever back out in cases of written communication.
- ✓ Emails are an important way of communication at the workplace. All the employees who ought to be a part of the communication should be kept in the loop. The emails should be self-explanatory and provide common information to all.
- ✓ The superiors must be accessible to all the members and lend a sympathetic ear in cases of queries.
- ✓ Effective communication plays an important role in increasing the morale of the employees.

Relationship

The employees must avoid conflicts and disagreements at the workplace as it lead to no solution.

- ✓ Don't find faults in your fellow workers. One should be a little more flexible and understanding.
- ✓ Your colleagues can be your friends also; after all you spend the maximum time at the workplace. Don't always think that your colleagues would do harm to you.
- ✓ Avoid controversies and rumours at the workplace.
- ✓ One should always work with an open mind. Don't drag issues unnecessarily at workplace.
- ✓ Accept the challenges with a smile.
- ✓ Go out once in a while with your colleagues for dinners, small get-togethers and parties. Such activities help in breaking the ice and also promote a healthy culture at the workplace.
- ✓ Celebrate important festivals at the workplace for a positive work culture.

    ✓ Whenever possible, help your colleagues.

- **Setbacks of Organization Culture**
  What is Organization ?

A common platform where individuals from different backgrounds, mentalities, educational qualifications, interests and attitudes come together to work towards a goal as well as earn bread and butter for themselves is called an organization. Every organization has a unique style of working often called its culture.

Culture - The ideologies, beliefs and policies of an organization form its culture.

It is essential for the employees to adjust well in the culture of the organization for them to deliver their level best. However it has been observed that in certain cases the employees might find themselves in trouble whenever there is a change in the work culture. The work culture instead of giving the employees a sense of direction might become a burden for them. The first and the foremost problem which arises out of a set work culture is adjustment.

- **Setbacks of an organization culture**

The culture of an organization is not formed in a single day. A culture is the cumulative outcome of the interaction amongst the employees and their behavioural patterns at the workplace. A culture is formed when individuals follow certain values and adhere to guidelines over a considerable period of time. Problems arise when new employees step into the shoes of the existing ones and take charge. They bring new ideas, new plan of actions and new concepts along with them and thus cause problems for the existing employees. They tend to hire their own people and eventually side-line the current employees.

    ✓ Adjustment problems arise when new joinees find it difficult to adjust to the prevailing work culture. They find it difficult to concentrate and tend to lose interest in work. For them the work becomes a burden and they simply attend office to earn money. They never get attached to their workplace.

    ✓ Culture in certain cases can also become a liability to an organization. Strict policies and harsh rules can sometimes create problems for the employees and they find it difficult to stick to the organization for a long time. Retaining the employee becomes a nightmare in cases of weak cultures. The policies must be employee friendly and benefit one and all. An organization where male employees dominate the female counterparts follow a culture where late sitting is a regular feature. Male individuals might find this kind of culture extremely comfortable but a female employee would not be able to adjust well in such a culture. The youngsters would have a problem in organizations where the older generation decides the policies and forms the culture.

✓ An individual working in any particular culture for quite some time would develop certain habits and mindset. It is not easy to get rid of a habit all of sudden. Difficulties arise whenever employees wish to move on for better opportunities. The new organization might not promise them the same facilities and comforts which their previous organization offered. The incentive plan in this organization might not be as lucrative as it was in the previous organization.

Example: Janet worked with an organization where the employees had the liberty to reach office as per their convenience. Her current organization followed a strict culture where the management was particular about the work timings, hence causing problems for Janet as she was used to flexible timings.

✓ An employee finds it difficult to implement new ideas and concepts in a culture which has been practised for several years. For him the culture becomes a limitation, where he has to work as per the set guidelines and predefined policies.

✓ One should always remember that no culture is more important than employees. They are the true assets of an organization. The work culture should never bind the employees to do something innovative.

- **Threats to Organization Culture**
  What do you understand by Organization culture?

Organization culture reflects the working conditions, behaviour of employees, their thought processes, beliefs and so on. Organization culture in a layman's language is often called as work culture and plays an essential role in extracting the best out of employees. Work culture needs to be healthy for employees not only to enjoy their work but also deliver their level best and develop a feeling of loyalty and attachment towards their respective organizations.

Let us go through the threats to organization culture:

Negative attitude and ego are in fact two biggest threats to organization culture. Individuals who find it difficult to look at the brighter sides of life often crib and complain and spoil the entire work culture. They themselves hardly work and on top of it also influence others. Problems are in fact everywhere. Can you name one organization where there is absolutely no tension or stress? Believe me, you would find peculiar characters in every organization. You just need to know how to deal with them. How many organizations would you change? Employees who think that fighting is the only solution to solve issues are sadly mistaken and in fact pose a major threat to organization culture. Remember, strikes, unions, mass bunking not only spoil the organization culture but also bring a bad name to the organization. Develop a positive attitude and learn to ignore things if you really want your organization to do well and outshine its competitors.

There is no place of ego at workplace. Employees who carry their ego to work find it difficult to adjust with their fellow workers eventually affecting the work culture. In today's business scenario, people expect you to drop "Sir", "Maam" or "Boss" attached to a name in both written as well as verbal communication. Corporate culture gives you the liberty to address individuals by their first names only irrespective of position and age. Now, there are some individuals who would really not appreciate their juniors calling them by their names. You need to understand that there is nothing which is more important than your work and output. No individual would like to work in an environment where juniors are not treated with respect and care.

Would you ever like to leave an organization where all employees are treated as one? Ask yourself.

Favouritism is another big threat to work culture. Problems arise the moment you start giving special treatments to few employees. Do not favour someone just because he/she is your friend or you like the other person. Such behaviour is absolutely unacceptable and unethical .Favouritism not only spoils the work culture but also demotivates those who genuinely want to work and carve a niche for themselves. Employees who work hard need to be motivated and appreciated irrespective of their position in the hierarchy.

Lack of communication among employees is another major problem faced by organizations. Employees need to communicate with each other to discuss work, various issues and also reach to innovative solutions. Employees need to work as a single unit for better results. Bosses need to communicate effectively with their team members. Do not always expect your secretary to pass on information to your subordinates on your behalf. Let employees feel special. Treat them as indispensable resources of the organization.

Individuals taking their organizations for granted also spoil the work culture. You need to genuinely feel for your organization. A feeling of loyalty is essential. Don't work for anyone else but for yourself and obviously your organization. Things would never improve unless and until employees take pride in representing their respective organizations.

Open Door Policy - Meaning and its Advantages

An organization is a setup where individuals from diverse backgrounds, different educational qualifications, varied mentalities and temperaments join hands to work towards a common goal. It is the culture of the workplace which unites all the employees, help them enjoy their work and deliver their level best.

The values, policies, ideologies and beliefs of an organization form its culture. The culture of any work place decides the way employees behave with their fellow workers. The employees are the assets of an organization who must contribute effectively to achieve the targets within the desired time frame.

One should not treat his organization as a mere source of earning money. It is essential for an individual to prioritize his work over other things. The employees must have a cordial relation with their superiors and the management for smooth flow of information and better understanding at workplace. Transparency is essential at all levels in the hierarchy to avoid conflicts and unnecessary disagreements. No one should feel neglected at work. Problems arise when queries remain unattended and bosses do not have time for their team members.

To avoid the above situation, organizations have introduced a policy named "Open Door Policy"

What is Open Door Policy ?

According to open door policy, the doors of the offices of superiors or the management (including the CEO) must remain open for the employees to have an easy access in cases of queries. The team members should have the liberty to walk up to their team leaders and discuss issues with them on an open forum.

The role of the managing director, chief executive officer or the chairman is not just to sit in locked cabins the entire day and shout on the employees; instead they should act as a strong pillar of support for them. A healthy interaction amongst the employees is essential for a positive ambience at the workplace. The management must address the employees from time to time to motivate them and expect the best out of them.

Advantages of an Open Door Policy

✓ Open door policy encourages effective communication between the employee and the management. The employees do not feel left out at the workplace as they know there is someone to support them always at the time of crisis. This way they get attached to the management and are always loyal towards the organization.

✓ There is no room for confusion when the employees directly interact with their superiors. They feel motivated and strive hard to live up to the expectations of the management. They never badmouth the management or their organization.

✓ Open door policy encourages healthy discussion at the workplace. Individuals exchange ideas and come to an innovative solution benefitting all. The employees are free to discuss their ideas with the superiors and gain from their talent and mentoring.

✓ Gone are the days when people used to fear their bosses. The "Hitler approach" does not work in the current scenario. The management must respect the decisions of the employees to expect the same in return. The management must make the employees feel indispensable for the organization and should lend a sympathetic ear whenever required.

✓ The open door policy enables the employees to seek their boss's help and freely discuss things with them for better clarity. Open door policy is essential for effective communication, proper feedbacks and better output. With the help of the open door policy, the employees do not crib amongst themselves, rather talk to their superiors, clear all their doubts and look forward towards a long term association with the organization.

Edgar Schein Model of Organization Culture

The term "Organization culture" refers to the values and beliefs of an organization. The principles, ideologies as well as policies followed by an organization form its culture. It is the culture of the workplace which decides the way individuals interact with each other and behave with people outside the company. The employees must respect their organization's culture for them to deliver their level best and enjoy their work. Problems crop up when individuals are unable to adjust to a new work culture and thus feel demotivated and reluctant to perform.

Who is Edgar Schein ?

Edgar Henry Schein born in 1928 is a renowned professor at the MIT Sloan School of Management who has studied extensively in the field of organization management.

- **Edgar Schein model of organization culture**

According to Edgar Schein - Organizations do not adopt a culture in a single day, instead it is formed in due course of time as the employees go through various changes, adapt to the external environment and solve problems. They gain from their past experiences and start practicing it everyday thus forming the culture of the workplace. The new employees also strive hard to adjust to the new culture and enjoy a stress free life.

Schein believed that there are three levels in an organization culture.

1. Artifacts

The first level is the characteristics of the organization which can be easily viewed, heard and felt by individuals collectively known as artifacts. The dress code of the employees, office furniture, facilities, behavior of the employees, mission and vision of the organization all come under artifacts and go a long way in deciding the culture of the workplace.

Organization A
- No one in organization A is allowed to dress up casually.
- Employees respect their superiors and avoid unnecessary disputes.
- The individuals are very particular about the deadlines and ensure the tasks are accomplished within the stipulated time frame.

Organization B
- The employees can wear whatever they feel like.
- Individuals in organization B are least bothered about work and spend their maximum time loitering and gossiping around.
- The employees use derogatory remarks at the work place and pull each other into controversies.

In the above case, employees in organization A wear dresses that exude professionalism and strictly follow the policies of the organization. On the other hand, employees in organization B have a laid back attitude and do not take their work seriously. Organization A follows a strict professional culture whereas Organization B follows a weak culture where the employees do not accept the things willingly.

2.   Values

The next level according to Schein which constitute the organization culture is the values of the employees. The values of the individuals working in the organization play an important role in deciding the organization culture. The thought process and attitude of employees have deep impact on the culture of any particular organization. What people actually think matters a lot for the organization? The mindset of the individual associated with any particular organization influences the culture of the workplace.

3.   Assumed Values

The third level is the assumed values of the employees which can't be measured but do make a difference to the culture of the organization. There are certain beliefs and facts which stay hidden but do affect the culture of the organization. The inner aspects of human nature come under the third level of organization culture. Organizations where female workers dominate their male counterparts do not believe in late sittings as females are not very comfortable with such kind of culture. Male employees on the other hand would be more aggressive and would not have any problems with late sittings. The organizations follow certain practices which are not discussed often but understood on their own. Such rules form the third level of the organization culture.

Robert A Cooke Model of Organization Culture

Individuals from different backgrounds and varied interests come together on a common platform called organization to achieve targets as well as earn bread and butter for themselves. Individuals work in unison towards a common goal. The behaviour of the employees to a large extent depends on the culture of the workplace.

How people interact amongst themselves and with outsiders also depend on the organization culture.

The policies, practices, principles of an organization form its culture. It is essential for an employee to understand the culture and adjust to it well to deliver his level best and win management's appreciation.

Robert A Cooke proposed the following model of organization culture.

Every employee has a way of behaving at the workplace which he feels is the correct way and would help him survive in the organization for a longer duration. Such perceptions of employees form the culture of the organization. According to Robert A Cooke, the culture of an organization is the way employees behave at the workplace to ensure stable future and growth.

Cooke proposed three types of culture in the organization:

1.   Constructive Culture

There are certain organizations which encourage healthy interaction amongst the employees. The individuals have the liberty to share their ideas, exchange information and discuss things to come to an innovative solution beneficial to all. Conflicts arise when employees feel neglected and are not allowed to speak their minds. People crib amongst themselves when queries remain unattended leading to severe demotivation. A constructive culture encourages discussions and exchange of ideas amongst employees. Constructive culture motivates the employees and eventually extracts the best out of them.

The key features of a constructive culture are:

- Achievement: A constructive culture helps the employees to achieve the targets within the stipulated time frame.
- Self Actualizing: In this kind of culture, an employee stays motivated and realizes his full potential.
- Encouragement: A Constructive culture encourages employees to deliver their level best and strive hard for furthering the image of the organization.

- Affiliative: The employees avoid conflicts and unnecessary disputes and promote a positive ambience at the workplace.

2.   Passive Culture

In a passive culture, the employees behave in a way contrary to the way they feel is correct and should be the ideal way. In a passive culture, the main motive of the employee is to please the superiors and make his position safe and secure in the organization. In such a culture, employees unhappily adhere to the guidelines and follow the rules and regulations just to save their job.

The characteristics of a passive culture are:

✓ Approval: In such a culture employees can't take decisions on their own. They need to take their boss's approval before implementing any idea.

✓ Conventional: Employees are bound by rules and regulations of the organization and act according to the prescribed standards only.

✓ Dependent: In such a culture, the performance of the employees is dependent on the superior's decisions and they blindly follow their boss's orders.

✓ Avoidance: Employees tend to avoid their own personal interests, satisfaction and simply act according to the company's policies.

3.   Aggressive Culture

Organizations following an aggressive culture promote competition amongst the employees. They encourage the employees to compete against each other so that each one performs better than his fellow worker. In such a culture, employees seeking their colleague's assistance are often called as incompetent employees. Every individual vies for power, attention and strive hard to win appreciation.

The key features of such a culture are:

✓ Opposition
✓ Power
✓ Perfectionist

✓ Competitive

In the above culture, employees are aggressive, compete against each other and try to become perfectionist by identifying their mistakes and eventually minimizing them.

- **Hofstede Model of Organization Culture**

Organization culture refers to the various ideologies, beliefs and practices of an organization which make it different from others. The culture of any workplace decides how employees would behave with each other or with the external parties and also decide their involvement in productive tasks.

Hofstede also known as Geert Hofstede proposed that national and regional factors contribute to the culture of the organization and eventually influence the behaviour of employees in the organization.

According to Hofsteide there are majorly five factors which influence the culture of the workplace.

1.   Power Distance

Organization A

The power was distributed equally among all irrespective of their designations. Every individual regardless of his level in the hierarchy enjoyed equal benefits and rights.

Organization B

In organization B the superiors enjoyed a special treatment from the management and the team leaders were delegated more responsibilities as compared to the team members.

Power distance index refers to the differences in the work culture as per the power delegated to the employees. There are some organizations which believe in appointing team leaders or team managers who are responsible for their respective teams and have the challenge of extracting the best out of the members. The team members also have to respect their team leaders and work as per their orders and advice.

However in some organizations, every employee is accountable for his own performance. No special person is assigned to take charge of the employees. The individuals are answerable to none except for themselves. Every employee gets an equal treatment from the management and has to take ownership of his /her own work.

2.   Masculinity vs. Feminity

This refers to the effect of differences in male and female values on the culture of the organization. Organizations where male employees dominate their female counterparts will follow different policies as compared to organizations where females have a major say in the decision making process of the organization. Male employees would be more aggressive as compared to the females who would be more caring and softhearted. The responsibilities also vary as per the sex of the employees. The female employees are never assigned something which requires late sittings or frequent travellings.

3.   Individualism

There are some organizations which strongly rely on team work. Here individuals with a common interest come together and work in unison as a team. These organizations believe that the output is always more when individuals exchange their ideas, discuss things among themselves to come out with innovative ideas. In such a scenario the employees share a healthy relationship and take each other's help when required.

However certain organizations follow a culture where individuals do not believe in working as a single unit and prefer working individually.

4.   Uncertainty Avoidance Index

Uncertainty avoidance index refers to a culture where employees know how to respond to unusual and unforeseen circumstances. It deals with the tolerance level of the employees in both comfortable and uncomfortable situations. Organizations try hard to avoid such situations and also prepare the employees to adjust well in all conditions.

5.   Long Term Orientation

There are some organizations which focus on long term relationship with the employees. In such organizations people have a steady approach and strive hard to live up to the expectations of the management. Employees get attached to the organization and do not look at short term objectives. On the contrary, some organizations have employees who are more concerned with their position and image. They follow a culture where people move on in a short span of time and nothing is done to retain them. The employees are concerned only with their profits and targets and leave as and when they get a better opportunity.

Charles Handy Model of Organization Culture

What is an organization ?

An organization is a setup where individuals (employees) come together to work for a common goal. It is essential for the employees to work in close coordination, deliver their level bests and achieve the targets within the stipulated time frame for the smooth functioning of the organization.

Every organization has certain values and follows some policies and guidelines which differentiate it from others. The principles and beliefs of any organization form its culture. The organization culture decides the way employees interact amongst themselves as well as external parties. No two organizations can have the same culture and it is essential for the employees to adjust well in their organization's culture to enjoy their work and stay stress-free.

Several models have been proposed till date explaining the organization culture, one of them being the Charles Handy model.

Who is Charles Handy ?

Charles Handy born in 1932 in Ireland is a well-known philosopher who has specialized in organization culture.

According to Charles Handy's model, there are four types of culture which the organizations follow:

Let us understand them in detail:

1.   Power

There are some organizations where the power remains in the hands of only few people and only they are authorized to take decisions. They are the ones who enjoy special privileges at the workplace. They are the most important people at the workplace and are the major decision makers. These individuals further delegate responsibilities to the other employees. In such a culture the subordinates have no option but to strictly follow their superior's instructions. The employees do not have the liberty to express their views or share their ideas on an open forum and have to follow what their superior says. The managers in such a type of culture sometimes can be partial to someone or the other leading to major unrest among others.

2.   Task Culture

Organizations where teams are formed to achieve the targets or solve critical problems follow the task culture. In such organizations individuals with common interests and specializations come together to form a team. There are generally four to five members in each team. In such a culture every team member has to contribute equally and accomplish tasks in the most innovative way.

3.   Person Culture

There are certain organizations where the employees feel that they are more important than their organization. Such organizations follow a culture known as person culture. In a person culture, individuals are more concerned about their own self rather than the organization. The organization in such a culture takes a back seat and eventually suffers. Employees just come to the office for the sake of money and never get attached to it. They are seldom loyal towards the management and never decide in favour of the organization. One should always remember that organization comes first and everything else later.

4.   Role culture

Role culture is a culture where every employee is delegated roles and responsibilities according to his specialization, educational qualification and interest to extract the best out of him. In such a culture employees decide what best they can do and willingly accept the challenge. Every individual is accountable for something or the other and has to take ownership of the work assigned to him. Power comes with responsibility in such a work culture.

- **Introduction to Organizational Diversity**

We often hear the term "diversity" bandied about in our everyday usage. Usually, when we come across the term, it is in the context of having a mix of gender, race, ethnic, sexual orientation etc in a setting wherein there is no discrimination based on these traits.

In an organizational context, diversity refers to equality of opportunity and employment without any bias because of these traits. Indeed, it has become fashionable in the present scenario to have a diverse mix of employees drawn from all classes and proclivities so that the aura of correctness and humanitarianism can be actualized. However, this does not mean that organizational diversity has succeeded or it has become the norm in organizations. Rather, there are many barriers to diversity even after strenuous efforts by activists and experts and these relate to societal mindsets and personal psychological discomfort with having people drawn from diverse backgrounds working alongside.

In the United States, the government encourages and mandates organizational diversity as a matter of law and even to the extent of ensuring that, corporates not only follow the letter of the law but also the spirit of the law. This is reflected in the equal opportunity employer law, which states that organizations cannot discriminate against potential job applicants on race, gender, ethnicity, nationality, and sexual orientation. As we shall discuss in subsequent, each of these characteristics sets apart people from each other and hence there needs to be a mindset change apart from brining in laws that would make acceptance of diversity that much easier.

In other parts of the world, diversity is not practiced in society and let alone organizations which make a feeble attempt to enforce the rules. The reason for this is the prevailing cultural attitudes against certain sections of society, which makes it impossible for corporates to embrace diversity since they risk the wrath of the dominant cultural and societal groups. The point here is that when the entire society discriminates against say, homosexuals or lesbians, it is indeed difficult for even the best meaning of corporate leaders to buck this trend.

Hence, it needs to be remembered that organizational diversity is not only about a certain organization's policies but also reflects the broader societal consensus on this issue.

Of course, this is not to say since society discriminates against ethnic minorities, corporates can do so likewise. On the other hand, there is more responsibility on corporates to follow their heart and heed their conscience and ensure that their organizations reflect diversity. The point here is that there is a symbiotic relationship between organizations and their environment and hence both must work in tandem to resolve cultural conflicts and biases. When either is unwilling for whatever reasons, leaders must step in and ensure that diversity is encouraged for humanity's sake. This is the way shown by several business leaders like NR Narayana Murthy of Infosys and the late legendary Steve Jobs of Apple who put their personal reputations at stake to promote diversity.

- **Benefits of Organizational Diversity**

Why do you think an individual is recruited? Is it because he/she is qualified enough to do justice to a particular role or he/she belongs to the religion you belong? The answer is very simple. Obviously an individual is hired because the company feels that he/she can contribute to his/her level best towards achieving organization goals. Discriminating someone on the basis of his/her religion, caste, background or community at workplace is absolutely unethical.

Let us go through the benefits of organizational diversity:

Organizational diversity brings together individuals of varied experiences, educational qualifications, age groups and backgrounds at a common place - your organization. The first and the foremost benefit of organizational diversity is individuals get to learn lots of things from each other. You get to know about each other's religion, community and also get an opportunity to gain from each other's expertise. You might not know everything which probably someone associated with the organization for quite some time would know. It is foolish to underestimate anyone.

Organization A had individuals who were more than forty years of age and were in the system say for last ten years. The management did not like the idea of recruiting fresh talent and relied only on experienced ones. In due course of time, the experienced lot could not cope up with the changing technologies and failed to survive the challenging times. Organization A eventually suffered great losses and had to be shut down.

Organization B on the other hand believed in the concept of organizational diversity and had individuals of all age groups, work experiences, qualifications striving for a common goal. Young talents are generally little keener on upgrading their knowledge as compared to older employees who are on the verge of retirement. During tough times, Organization B gained not only from the experiences of the older people but also from the young lot who faced challenges with a smile and encouraged others to stay calm and patient.

An organization needs to have all types of people around. Everyone is talented and everyone if mentored and guided well can actually make a difference. So what if the other person is a fresher? If he/she has the right knowledge, he/she can actually prove to be an asset for your organization.

Organizational diversity ensures equal opportunities for all. What is the problem in recruiting female employees? Why are they denied top level positions? Just because they are little sensitive. Trust me; no one would buy this logic in today's professional world. It is high time when male employees start taking their female counter parts seriously and provide them their due credit. Anyone who has the talent and passion to make it big in the professional world ought to get an opportunity to showcase his/her talent. Organizations eventually benefit from the innovate ideas of all individuals when pooled together.

Organizational diversity goes a long way in exposing individuals to varied cultures and traditions. It gives you a chance to know about other festivals and how they are being celebrated by other religions. Believe me, during festival seasons, everyone loves to bring delicacies from home and it is like a big party at workplace. Organizational diversity not only brings employees closer to each other but also strengthens the bond among them. Employees feel happy and motivated when they celebrate different festivals together. This certainly also reflects in their work when they readily help each other and seldom indulge in unnecessary conflicts and solve issues among themselves. Individuals from different backgrounds and experiences can also sit together, brainstorm ideas and reach to better solutions benefitting the organization.

- **Role of Management in Managing Organizational Diversity**

Organizational diversity enables individuals from diverse backgrounds, religions, communities, age groups, experiences, educational qualifications and so on to work on a common platform, striving hard towards achieving the goals and objectives of the organization within the shortest possible time frame.

Management plays an essential role in managing organizational diversity:

All individuals need to be treated equally. If you have recruited someone, he/she is your employee and thus indispensable resource of the organization. Do not misbehave once he/she joins. You have no rights to ill treat the other individual just because he is a peon. Management should not forget that even the office boy is an employee of the organization and ought to be treated with utmost respect and care, the same way you treat your other employees. Make them feel important. Do not make separate policies for them. Remember, even they have the right to enjoy company's benefits, the way others do.

Every employee is important irrespective of designation; amount of time spent in the organization or educational qualification and contributes in his/her own way. Organization B had all types of employees, some who recently joined and some who were there in the system for quite some time. Joe was never called for team meetings because he joined the organization just one month back. This certainly is a wrong practice. Management and superiors need to ensure that every individual is called for team meetings and also has the liberty to contribute in formulating team strategies and organization policies.

Remember, an organization does not always need experienced people but also young and dynamic individuals who have the passion for innovation and accepting challenges. Do not neglect someone just because he is new to the industry. You never know when he comes up with a wonderful idea which would benefit not only the team but the entire organization.

Appraisals and incentive plans need to be similar for everyone. If you have decided for twenty percent hike, make sure it is same for everyone, be it the general manager, manager, executive or the office boy. Even the office boy has the right to ask for his appointment letter. It is his right. Appraisals should be strictly done based on individual's performance over a period of year and nothing else.

Encourage effective communication at the workplace. No employee should be left out of important discussions. Management needs to ensure transparency at all levels of hierarchy. This is in fact the best way to effectively manage organizational diversity.

You really need to take good care of your female employees to promote a healthy work culture. Ensure your male employees are not misbehaving with their female counterparts and if they do so, you need to take strict action immediately. Do not ask your female employees to work till late unless and until there is an emergency and you have a deadline to follow. If you have asked them to do so, make sure you arrange a cab to drop them home. Ask your administration department to make proper arrangements for them if they need to travel out of the city.

It is the responsibility of the management to encourage individuals to celebrate and enjoy all festivals irrespective of their religion and community. We may be Hindu, Muslim, Sikh or Christian, but above all we are Indians. Do not be happy because 25th December is a holiday and you will have another day to watch your favourite movie or spend some time with your family. Do celebrate all festivals and enjoy them to the fullest. Do not ignore someone just because he/she does not belong to your religion. Believe me, individuals who do so have no rights to be a part of the system.

Organizational Diversity: Ideal vs Practice

The previous one introduced the concept of organizational diversity and how the various supporting laws and regulations square up against organizational commitment. This one looks at how the ideals of organizational diversity measure up to the practice of diversity across the world.

As with any idealistic notion, organizational diversity is usually done more in theory than in practice if the experiences of organizations in the United States and Asia are taken into reckoning. This is because the concept is good in theory where all organizations commit themselves to employing people of all genders, classes, ethnicities and sexual orientation.

However, due to prevailing mindsets, organizations do not actually practice this ideal and often the result is that organizations pay lip service to the ideal of diversity without practicing it. This results in the organizations proclaiming their commitment but in a hypocritical manner, abandoning it for the sake of convenience.

In India, Infosys was one of the first companies to have introduced the IWIN (Infosys Women's Inclusivity Network) initiative where the management proclaimed their support for diversity. However, with the passage of time, the initiative was suitably toned down to meet business goals where the need to encourage diversity was given up at the altar of convenience. Though the initiative had the blessings of the founders including NR Narayana Murthy, other executives at different levels did not see the need to follow these principles because of mindset issues. The point here is that mindsets are hard to change and hence, diversity is often sacrificed for organizational cohesion. The usual excuse given is that there are not enough employable candidates from different backgrounds and hence, it is not possible to practice diversity. However, a careful consideration of the facts shows that this is not true given the available labor pool that is very rich in diversity.

Further, diversity also means that the employees from different orientations are treated equally with other employees and inclusivity is practiced. Often, it is the case that employees from different backgrounds are hired and then treated shabbily because their coworkers have different views about diversity than the management. The reason for elucidating the point so deeply is that unless mindsets change, diversity would remain a concept on paper only. Hence, the only way out for companies to embrace diversity would be to educate their employees and enforce strict codes of conduct across the organization. Only then would the employees from different orientations would feel comfortable working in the company. In this endeavor, the government has to do its bit by passing and enforcing laws that take care of the rights of the differently abled and differently oriented employees.

The inescapable conclusion is that unless there is a wholesome embrace of diversity by walking the talk instead of talking the talk, diversity would only remain compliant with the letter of the law and not the spirit of the law. This is the overriding message that emerges after surveying the experiences of organizations worldwide and in Asia.

- **Diversity and Inclusivity as a Value Based Imperative**

Diversity and inclusivity in organizations have to be practiced instead of being preached. This is because they are concepts that lend credence to value based management and management that is humanistic in nature. Many organizations claim to have diversity programs only to have a few women in positions of power or differently abled employees just for the sake of satisfying the principle of diversity in the letter of the law rather than the spirit of the law. This is the case with many top-notch companies where regressive attitudes exist to prevent women and other minorities from being significant. However, this is neither the ideal situation nor even the acceptable situation, as management has to be driven by values instead of being driven by profit alone. Hence, there is a need to practice value-based management and incorporate diversity as a guiding principle for recruitment and promotions.

Of course, we are not making the case for an affirmative action kind of scenario where disadvantaged groups are recruited and promoted irrespective of their abilities. Rather the point that is being made here is that there should not be implicit and explicit barriers to women and differently abled employees reaching senior positions.

The prevailing attitudes must change and leadership must set an example to the rest of the organization to follow when formulating and actualizing diversity management policies and procedures. In this scenario, women and differently abled people as well as disadvantaged groups are treated equally with the other employees and without showing them undue favours, barriers are not placed in their path. This should be the goal of diversity management if value based management is adopted as the guiding principle for organizations.

The point here is that the ongoing economic crisis has shown how lack of ethics and normative principles can wreak havoc with the corporate system. Hence, the only way out is for corporate leaders to practice value based management and this can be done only if the senior leadership walks the talk instead of just talking the talk. Moreover, a culture of tolerance and inclusivity has to be built into the organizational DNA since senior management alone cannot change the system on their own. What this means is that middle management and even the employees from the ground up have to be taught to respect diversity and welcome inclusivity.

There are many companies including Infosys where the senior management is committed to diversity and inclusivity but the situation in the shop floor is something different altogether. Indeed, there are many instances of employees showing scant respect for diversity and be exclusive in their dealings with women. This presents problems for the companies concerned, as not only does this attitude vitiate the organizational culture but is also detrimental for its reputation and adherence to corporate governance principles. As mentioned earlier, if there is one lesson from the recent events, it is that one can fool people for some time but not all the time. Hence, value based management that promotes diversity and inclusivity as a business principle should be the goal of corporate leaders.

- ### Fostering an Inclusive Environment

The question that is uppermost on business leaders' mind is how to foster an inclusive environment as the current environment in the business world is about not tolerating harassment and discrimination. For instance, in recent years, there has been some high profile cases involving senior management figures in the US and in India in matters related to sexual harassment and discrimination. Though the defendants and the victims reached out of court settlements in some cases, the damage done to the reputations of individuals and the companies is immense. This makes the case for fostering an inclusive environment in the workplace and avoiding such incidents that much more important.

It needs to be remembered that having policies in place alone is not enough to prevent harassment. Rather, companies and business leaders must walk the talk and practice what they preach about having an inclusive environment in the workplace.

The first aspect here is the sensitization towards gender, ethnic, and alternative sexualities and orientations that must take place before any meaningful action on inclusivity happens. For this to be actualized, employees at all levels have to be made sensitive to the problems of women, racial minorities, and those who are of alternative sexual orientation. In many multinationals, explicit training programs are conducted to sensitize the staff on these issues. This is a practice that other companies can follow to have an inclusive environment. Apart from this, there needs to be redressal mechanisms wherein victims can report the incident in a confidential and secure manner. This means that the identity of the victim is kept confidential until the incident is investigated and action taken.

The other aspect is that strict punishment must be meted out in case wrongdoing is proved. Instead of mildly reprimanding the perpetrator and allowing the person to get away with the misdemeanor, there needs to be concrete action so that such incidents are not allowed to recur again. The point here is that justice must be seen to be done as well as seen to be effective. In many organizations, there are no punitive actions taken against the perpetrators, which embolden them and others to repeat such acts. Hence, the only way out would be for the company to initiate as strict an action possible that would deter others and serve as an example.

Finally, change comes from within and there is no point in having rules and regulations as well as punishments if the underlying mindset is one of mediaevalist thinking. Hence, the best way to foster inclusive working environment would be to effect a change in the mindset that creates inclusivity rather than narrow mindedness. Therefore, it would be in the interests of business leaders if they inculcated some of the values like tolerance, respect, and diversity among the staff. Only when there is an attitudinal change can there is an inclusive working environment.

In conclusion, fostering an inclusive working environment takes time, patience, and courage which the business leaders' and the other management figures need to have in abundance.

- **Communicating Across Cultures**

In these times when global corporations operate in many countries across the world, it is important for the employees in these organizations to know the nuances of intercultural communication. It is often the case that many Asian employees (especially the younger lot) say, "they passed out in a certain year from college". This has different connotations in the West as it refers to the act of losing consciousness. The correct phrase would be that "we graduated". To take another example, it is common for many Westerners to start talking about the weather as an icebreaker for the conversation. However, this is interpreted differently in Asian countries where many employees do not seem to understand why the weather is a topic for conversation. Finally, many Asian employees (especially Indians) usually use the term "freaked out" to mean that they have had a good time. However, this is interpreted differently in the US where it has entirely different connotations.

The point here is that intercultural communication depends on a variety of factors that include the specifics of language, style, and substance.

Further, one has to be sensitive to the fact that what is acceptable in one culture might be prohibited in another culture. Hence, it is common for Asian employees to enquire about the families of their coworkers, whereas, in the West, it is not common for the employees to talk openly about them.

Most important aspect in cultural communication is the gender aspect where the way in which employees address the issues of women in the workplace makes a lot of difference to how they are interpreted. In the West, employees are usually politically correct in their communication, which means that they do not overly make racist and gender based statements. This does not mean that such issues do not exist there. On the contrary, there are enough cases of sexual harassment at the workplace in the west. Rather, the point is that in the West, employees are usually guarded when talking about their female coworkers. However, many Asian employees are openly racist and gender biased in their comments.

The other aspect of cross-cultural communication is the issue of how cultural differences are handled. For instance, while it is common for Asians to know many details about the US and the Europe, many westerners have a rather sketchy knowledge of countries other than in the West. This ignorance can sometimes be annoying to the Indians as was evident in the recent issue involving the popular Talk Show Host, Oprah Winfrey. Her statement that "Indians still eat with their hands" kicked up a row with many Indians taking umbrage at this remark. Hence, one must be cognizant of cultural differences and not say or do anything that would be interpreted in a different manner. Finally, cross-cultural communication is all about sensitivity and having empathy with the person from the other culture. Hence, it goes beyond differences and depends largely on the individual who is communicating.

In conclusion, there is a need for training for employees who are being sent onsite or who have to deal with employees from other cultures. This would make the job of communicating across cultures easier and would reduce the chances for faux pas in the communication process.

- **Intercultural Communication: The Hofstede Model**

One of the most widely used frameworks for analyzing cultural differences is the model developed by the eminent cultural theorist, Geert Hofstede. In this model, the differences in culture between countries have been plotted along five dimensions, which can be used as the basis for predicting the cultural differences between different countries. The model was developed after extensive research into the cultural differences between different countries and after surveys of thousands of employees in the West and the East. The five dimensions along which the cultural differences are plotted are power distance, masculinity vs. femininity, long-term orientation vs. short-term thinking, individualism vs. collectivism, and uncertainty avoidance. The model is comprehensive and exhaustive in its treatment of cultural differences across cultures.

To take the first dimension, power distance measures the extent to which hierarchy dominates the work environment. In the US, the power distance is relatively small when compared to China where the power distance is more because of the hierarchical nature of Chinese society. Similarly, the Masculine traits predominate in India and China as compared to the US and UK as the cultures in the former tends towards patriarchy.

The third dimension of individualism vs. collectivism yields the result that employees in the West would be highly individualistic as compared to the employees in the East who subscribe to the group instead of to the individual. The fourth dimension of long-term thinking vs. short-term thinking is likewise different in the US and the UK where the emphasis is on getting the short-term results whereas in China and India, there is a tendency to look ahead into the future. Finally, the fifth dimension of uncertainty avoidance refers to the structured work environment, which in the West would be oriented towards specific and measurable goals and objectives whereas out of the box thinking is prevalent in the East.

The Hofstede model is useful for expatriate managers who when they work in the East find it easy to understand the cultural differences in the work environment. Using this model, the expatriate managers can be trained to adjust to the different cultures. To take an example, it is common in the East (China and India) to be hierarchical in the organizational structure where the position and the status of the employee matters a lot. Given the fact that in the West, these are important but not to the extent that they are in the East, expatriate managers can learn to negotiate cultural differences using this model. Another important aspect is that culturally China and India are male dominated, which is different from the US, and the UK where gender equality is prevalent. Hence, the expatriate managers can likewise adjust to the East when they work there using this model.

Finally, for expatriate managers to adjust to the local cultures, adopting a "Glocal" approach would be the ideal solution. This approach wherein a global outlook is combined with a local approach means that multinationals can adapt themselves to the local cultures and at the same time do not lose focus of their global vision. This is the most important learning that the Hofstede model and the other models of culture provide to the expatriate managers. In conclusion, cultural differences can make or mar the chances of multinationals in the globalized world economy of the present. Hence, it is important to realize and understand that culture plays a prominent part in shaping the work environment.

- **Recruiting a Diverse Team**

    The previous one in this module discussed how diversity as a core value is important for organizations. We have also discussed how actualizing diversity means that the entire organization has to walk the talk instead of merely espousing it in name and then practicing something different altogether.

One of the most important actions that any organization can take is to ensure that diversity and inclusivity are inculcated right from the recruitment process itself. This means that recruiting a diverse is the first step towards realizing the goal of diversity. Though the governments in many countries including the US and India do not mandate a certain percentage of the employees to be women, racial minorities, or those with alternate sexual orientations, they do specify that equal opportunities must be given to everyone and that the organizations should not discriminate against anybody on these counts.

For instance, we often hear the term Organization X is an "equal opportunity employer". What this means is that the organization treats all potential recruits in the same manner and does not discriminate against them in any respect. However, announcing that we are equal to towards everybody does not that mean that we are equal towards everybody in practice. Take for example, the practice in many companies in India to recruit employees based on location and because of political pressures. Further, many companies in Asia do not recruit women for the jobs that need overseas travel or those jobs that have extended working hours. This certainly goes against the grain of diversity and hence must be avoided at all costs. Further, many companies go by the appearance of candidates and not necessarily by merit alone. Of course, we are not saying that for the jobs that need pleasant demeanor like Airline Stewards and Stewardess or jobs in the hospitality sectors, employers must not give importance to looks. Rather, what we are saying is that in general, it would be a good practice to recruit employees based on merit alone instead of other considerations.

The best way to recruit a diverse team is to have "blind resumes" where except for the qualifications of the candidate, nothing else is visible. In this scenario, the potential recruit can be a woman, racial minority, physically challenged or any of the other categories that comes under inclusivity. Therefore, the recruit has a fair chance to make it to the interview stage without any bias. Once the interview is announced, it would be better for the companies to have interviewers drawn from a heterogeneous group instead of having a homogenous group. This would ensure that the candidate is not discriminated against. Finally, it would be in the fitness of things if the candidate were not asked questions from where they are and their preferences about things other than work related matters alone. This is somewhat hard to actualize but is sorely needed if organizations have to recruit diverse teams.

It must be made clear to the hiring team that asking questions about matters that are not directly related to the job at hand is not allowed. Further, the HR representative and the manager in charge of the diversity program must be allowed a greater say in recruitment and preferably, present during the interview.

- **Managing Diversity at the Workplace**

The previous one in this module discussed the ways and means of attracting diversity and how to recruit diverse teams. This one discusses how to manage diverse teams and to ensure that diversity is actualized in practice as opposed to merely paying lip service to the concept. Many organizations proclaim that they are committed to diversity while in reality; the work culture in those organizations is parochial, gender insensitive, and racist.

Hence, it is imperative that organizations not only preach diversity but also practice it. The best way to start would be to sensitize the middle management and the layers below them to gender, racial, and alternative lifestyles. This can be done by a concerted action in the form of training sessions and workshops where the message of diversity is percolated down to the lower most levels. The point here is that unless diversity as a term is understood and practiced by the middle and lower level employees, the efforts of the top management would go down the drain.

In many organizations, it is common for the managers to discriminate against particular racial and ethnic employees because they would be playing favorites with those employees of their own kind. These needs to be avoided at all costs and the senior leadership should send an unambiguous message that discrimination and harassment would not be tolerated at any cost. Further, in Asian countries, it is often the habit that employees lapse into their own language without considering the implications that it would have on the employees who do not speak their language. These needs to be avoided at all costs as well and strict enforcement of the language of communication (whether it is local or global) must be done. The point here is that in many industries, the managers need to communicate in the language that the workers are comfortable with. Therefore, there are no issues in this case since the language of communication can vary. However, in corporate settings and in services sector companies, there are employees from diverse backgrounds who feel lost when the manager and the employees communicate in languages other than the official language of communication.

The next aspect is that the workplace must be gender sensitive, which means that managers and employees must not comment on matters that are sensitive to women. For instance, it is common in many organizations to pass overt and covert comments against women and to speak in demeaning ways. This must be avoided at all costs and we cannot emphasize more the importance of being gender sensitive at the workplace. The point here is that unless the work environment is free from gender stereotyping and racial and ethnic biases, the output from the organizations suffers.

Finally, as mentioned earlier, the senior leadership has to start with the middle management since they are the ones who deal with the boots on the ground and hence, they are in the best position to actualize gender and racial sensitivity. Unless the middle management is brought on board to actualize diversity, the workplace would remain insensitive and racist which definitely affects productivity.

- **Strategies for Organization Diversity**
  Let us go through few strategies for organizational diversity:
  Treat all individuals equally irrespective of their designation, back ground, community and religion. It hardly matters to the

organization whether the individual concerned is a Christian, Muslim, Hindu or a Sikh. What matters is his willingness to learn and passion to perform. Rules and regulations ought to be same for everyone. If the organization has decided to give ten leaves to its employees over a period of one year, make sure the same is granted to the office staff, pantry boy and even to the entry level executive. There are organizations where only the top level people enjoy the company benefits. Such a practice is unacceptable and leads to dissatisfaction among employees.

Incentive slabs and bonus criteria should not change with designation and hierarchy. Policies need to be same for every individual associated with the organization. If you scold your subordinate for coming late to work, make sure your top manager also comes on time. Don't change your policies for people.

Encourage employees to interact among themselves, discuss work, share experiences and also gain from each other's experience. Believe me, this way individuals not only come closer to each other but also get to know a lot about each other's strengths, culture, working style and also learn many new things from them. Every individual has some or the other talent. Let people share their knowledge with fellow workers and utilize their talent in the best possible way. Encourage them to sit with their fellow workers once every day to discuss team's strategies and even decide on the plan of action as to how to achieve the organization's goals within the shortest possible time frame. In today's business scenario, it is essential individuals develop the habit of working in unison; else work can never be accomplished within the deadlines. When individuals work together, not only they help each other in their respective assignments but also motivate each other to come up with their best work every time. This way, your organization also becomes a better place to work.

Appreciate employees whenever they do well. Individuals need to be given their due credit. Generally what happens is that whenever a team performs well, the team leader gets all the recognition and appreciation whereas the team members are left out. You need to be impartial towards your employees to promote organizational diversity.

Encourage individuals to celebrate festivals together irrespective of the religion and community they belong. Divide them in groups and ask them to decorate the office, arrange for a small party at office, get gifts for colleagues and so on. The idea is not to check whether they are capable of doing so or not but to make them aware of different cultures and traditions. Such an initiative also goes a long way in developing a feeling of trust and respect for their counter parts. This way, they start accepting each other and also working together as a single unit.

Encourage effective communication at the workplace to promote organizational diversity. Make sure everyone in the organization irrespective of his designation or level in the hierarchy is aware of his roles and responsibilities. Make sure organization policies are communicated well to each and everyone.

Guide your male employees and ask them to behave sensibly with their female counterparts. Make them understand that they need to draw a line somewhere while interacting with their female colleagues. Do not blindly support them. If any female employee complains about anyone, please do not ignore the same. Try to find out the actual problem and act at the earliest.

Make sure no individual gets undue advantage at the workplace.

- **The Business Case for Organizational Diversity**

The Business Case for Diversity

The module so far have focused on how organizational diversity makes eminent sense from legal compliance and value based perspectives. The discussion so far was about how organizations must embrace diversity as a value based imperative and for furthering corporate social responsibility.

This examines the business case for diversity and finds that not only do organizations have to pursue values they also have a strong business case for encouraging diversity. The reasons for this are to do with the increasingly heterogeneous nature of the customer base, the globalization imperative that makes diversity a precursor to growth, the looming talent crunch which translates into recruiting diverse teams as a way of avoiding it, and finally the changing imperatives of corporate leadership that confronts decision making in an increasingly uncertain world.

The Heterogeneous Nature of the Customer Base

It is no longer the case that the customers are made up of monolithic wholes that exhibit consistent and uniform patterns of behavior. On the other hand, the customer base for many companies has splintered into ethnic, racial, gender and other segmentations which means that organizations have to encourage diversity in their workforce to tackle the aspirations of the fragmented customer bases.

A New Mix of Employees is needed for Globalization

The fact that many companies are growing at scorching pace outside of the developed markets means that these companies need to have culturally, racially, and ethnically diverse employees in the target markets and hence they need to encourage diversity. The point here is that there is a premium on employees who can understand these markets better and hence there is a need for these employees to be recruited.

The Looming Talent Crunch

We had previously discussed how diversity casts the net wide and results in better talent. Combined with the looming talent crunch among the traditional employee segments, companies would be left with no choice but to recruit a workforce that is as diverse as possible and which results in the companies gaining competitive advantage over their rivals. The point here is that it is no longer values or CSR imperatives that drive diversity based practices. Instead, there is a compelling case to be made for economic and business imperatives as the drivers to encourage diversity.

- **The Changing Nature of Corporate Leadership**

Given the global odds that corporate leaders face in these times, decision-making is no longer linear or sequential and hence, the corporate leaders need to have as diverse a team as possible to ensure that they intuit and sense the market better than their competitors' sense. The need of the hour is to go beyond traditional notions of corporate leadership and instead, draw upon a set of diverse inputs and suggestions that encourage multiple views and multiple perspectives.

Finally, diversity is not only needed from legal and ethical or social expectations and instead, as this discussed; there are compelling business reasons for encouraging diversity. The point to be noted is that diversity makes for eminent business sense and hence, it must be hardwired into the organizational DNA. We shall discuss this in detail in subsequent one.

Lessons from Cutting Edge Research on Gender Diversity

Statistics show that only 49 percent of all Fortune 1000 companies have women on their senior management and that too restricted to one or two of them. This is also the case with 45 percent of boards that have minimal presence of women on the boards. However, recent cutting edge research has shown that the situation is likely to improve in the future because of some trends that are emerging. This is discusses some of the lessons that this research from the McKinsey Global Institute has uncovered and which can be put to use in organizations wishing for greater diversity.

Diversity is Encouraged by Personalities of Top Management

The research by the McKinsey Institute has shown that diversity is encouraged in those companies where the top management and the senior leadership shows a high level of commitment towards women empowerment and enabling women to perform according to their potential. There is also a cascading effect where having managers who are personally inclined to promote women often encourage women rather than those managers who have personality issues with respect to women. In short, diversity is encouraged in companies where the personalities of the managers are such that they often have firsthand experience of women playing a prominent role as opposed to managers who have chauvinistic attitudes towards women.

Organizational Culture Plays a Part in Promoting Diversity

Apart from the other aspects, the organizational culture and organizational DNA play an important role in promoting diversity as organizations that have embedded women's representation and women's empowerment as part of their organizational culture often seem to promote more women in the workplace as opposed to organizations that do not have a culture of respecting women. In brief, the core values and attitudes those organizations and their founders instill in the employees plays a major role in ensuring greater representation of women at all levels. Further, it is not enough for organizations to have gender diversity programs where the initial enthusiasm fades and reality bites if the culture and the core values that the organization lives with are not taken into account. This means that the vision and the mission that the company has and the push given to it by the founders matters a lot more than having diversity programs alone.

Systematic Improvements Must be Undertaken

Change is glacial and systematic change is more so. This means that there is a need to undertake multiyear diversity promotion programs that yield results after a few years instead of instantaneously. This also means that the gender diversity encouragement must be from all levels instead of just at a particular level and it must also be geared to ensure that the whole gamut of diversity promotion spanning all activities must be done. In other words, there needs to be a systemic effort to promote diversity and not individual contributions alone. This calls for an approach that spans divisions and levels and ensures that the message is sent out organization wide instead of being targeted at the micro level alone.

Diversity Must be Pushed from Above

The research has shown that diversity is "pushed" from above meaning that in those companies that have a higher proportion of women at the top, there tends to be greater involvement in encouraging diversity at all levels. Of particular importance is the fact that in those companies that have women board members, there are greater chances of the diversity culture percolating to the middle and bottom tiers as the women at the top take steps to ensure that women down the hierarchy are given a chance to progress. Moreover, women board members and in senior positions often mentor women at the lower levels leading to greater diversity all around.

Conclusion

Though the statistics are gloomy and paint a rather sorry picture of the current state of diversity programs, the research by McKinsey points to the future as being better in terms of diversity. This is because many organizations are applying these lessons in their internal processes and this means that going forward, we can expect more diversity in organizations.

The Practice of Organizational Diversity around the World

Organizational Diversity in the West

The practice of organizational diversity in contemporary organizations around the world offers some insights into how the discrimination, harassment, and prejudice based on gender and other minority groups plays itself out. For instance, in the West, it is common for employees to be politically correct in their utterances and communication with coworkers. This means that usually, one cannot expect racist and gender based remarks at the workplace. The ingrained sense of propriety and politically correct behavior means that senior management does not have to bother about the basics of organizational diversity and the practice of equal opportunity. For that matter, most western companies are equal opportunity employers where the clear organizational mandate is to ensure that the workplace is free from discrimination. Having said that, it must be noted that this does not mean that the west is free from sexual discrimination and harassment. On the contrary, despite the best efforts of the senior management, there are numerous cases of sexual discrimination and harassment directed towards women that often result in lengthy and expensive lawsuits against the companies. Indeed, in the recent past, even successful companies and investment banks have been the target of lawsuits and class action litigation in the US and in Europe.

Organizational Diversity in the East

On the other hand, in the East, one can expect the organizational culture to be hostile towards women. Without actually saying that the workplace culture is anti women, it needs to be mentioned that on several of the cultural parameters, it is often the case that workplaces in China, India, and other Asian countries tend to be patriarchic, male dominated, and discriminatory against women. Of course, the advent of the services sector and the concerted action by governments to discourage these tendencies partially as most service sector companies in the IT and BPO sectors have clear and stringent policies against discrimination and harassment. The key aspect here is that as Hofstede's cultural model shows, the impact of culture on the workplace environment is very high. Given the fact that the culture in many Asian countries is conservative and patriarchic, one can expect this aspect to have an effect on workplace behavior. Apart from this, the fact that many women in Asian companies put up with the discriminatory behavior because of the fear of stigma and going against the norm is a significant indicator the practice of organizational diversity in these companies.

- **Difference between East and the West**

The crucial difference between the practice of organizational diversity in the West and in the East is that whereas in the former, the cases of discrimination and harassment often end up in the courts, the tendency in Asian countries is to sweep these aspects under the carpet rather than taking action against the perpetrators. In the recent past, there have been a spate of cases in Asian companies where women have come out into the open and complained officially about discrimination and harassment. This is the result of greater awareness and concerted action by activists and governments that have been pressurized by the women's rights groups to take action against the offenders and ensure that discrimination and harassment do not become the norm rather than the exception. It is also the case that in China and India, strict anti harassment laws have been passed in the last year or so which would hopefully embolden women to report offences and instances of sexual harassment to the authorities. Some of the provisions in the laws that were passed include anonymous reporting, provision of a committee to look into the cases of harassment and discrimination, and stringent punishment by the companies to the offenders instead of just warning them and letting them off.

Closing Thoughts

Finally, it must be remembered that the practice of organizational diversity must come from within and not imposed from external factors. We can pass as many laws as possible but without a sea change in the attitudes of all the stakeholders, sexual discrimination and harassment would continue to haunt organizations and society.

Tips in Cross Cultural Management and Communications for those Traveling Overseas

In this globalized world, it has become the norm for many professionals to travel overseas on business assignments and for official meetings. This means that these professionals have to be sensitized to the different cultures and the customs of the countries to which they are travelling. This also calls for greater understanding of the cultural differences and an approach wherein the professionals would be able to mingle with their hosts in the country to which they are travelling easily and without creating any problems for either their companies or their hosts. For instance, many Asians travelling to the West have to understand that business meetings in the US and the UK represent formal affairs with set agendas and minutes being taken with little or no deviance from the agreed upon schedule. On the other hand, Westerners travelling to Asia and in particular, China are usually surprised by the freewheeling nature of the meetings and the rather omnibus nature of the discussions that are also meant to be knowledge sharing session where the Chinese try and elicit information about how the Western companies operates. Naturally, these differences lead to some hiccups between the parties and this is more the reason why

Westerners traveling to Asia and Asians travelling to the West have to be sensitized about the differences in culture and context.

Another aspect of this can be found in the attitudes towards women and minorities. In the US and the UK, one can expect the professionals to be politically correct in their words and deeds as far as women and minorities are concerned. This means that everyone tries to avoid overt and covert racism and gender discrimination apart from being non-controversial as far as other issues are concerned. On the contrary, Asians tend to be vocal about their opinions and attitudes and literally wear their views on their sleeves, which lead to awkward moments for Westerners in Asia and Asians in the West. Further, women are treated as equals in the West, the meetings are usually conducted in a formal and structured manner avoiding any racist, and gender related conversations. Apart from this, Westerners travelling to Asia and India, in particular are usually surprised by the sight of all the women employees sitting together during formal lunches and in some cases separately from the men and little or no mingling between the two groups. Of course, this is not to say that this is the norm but, in many cases, this happens leading to puzzlement and surprise among the Westerners. Moreover, the conversations with women employees are not informal and usually very stilted apart from the natural language barriers and the accent differences that accentuate the friction in cross cultural communication.

The third aspect of how professionals visiting other countries might need some background training is to do with how rules and regulations are observed in the countries they are visiting. For instance, many Asians travelling to the West are usually cautioned against breaking the law in even minor instances like over speeding or drinking and driving as well as having to show the identity for age proof when they have to buy alcohol or tobacco. Further, they are also advised to take medical insurance even for short trips because without insurance, it is difficult to get treatment in hospitals in the US. Even buying medicines is usually restricted to over the counter items and not prescription drugs that need doctor involvement. On the other hand, all these aspects are considered minor in Asian countries and hence, this is another significant cultural difference that has to be taken into account when professionals travel from the East to the West and vice versa.

Finally, though we have covered a few of the common instances of cultural differences, it is important to note that the best approach that anyone whether they travel from the West to the East or vice versa have to remember is that the people in the country they are visiting have to be treated according to how the visitor would like to be treated and hence, sensitivity and humanistic approaches would help everyone in the process.

- **Challenges in Organizational Diversity**

According to organizational diversity, individuals from diverse backgrounds, religions, communities, age groups, genders come together on a common platform to work towards a common goal - i.e. to achieve the objectives and targets of the organization within the shortest possible time frame. Organizational diversity ensures individuals with varied experiences; knowledge and expertise form a team and work together as a single unit.

Let us go through the challenges of organizational diversity:

The most common challenge of organizational diversity is lack of coordination among team members. Every individual has his/her own style of working. An individual who has just passed out of the college and started his career would be more aggressive and spontaneous than someone who is on the verge of retirement. Young professionals believe in meeting clients more often whereas the older lot believes in coordinating only through phone. They prefer sitting at office rather than going out and meeting people. That is where the problem arises.

A young professional would never understand and approve the working style of someone who is there in the system for say twenty five years and vice a versa. Difference in working style, attitude, temperament, belief lead to misunderstandings at the workplace. In such a situation, the team leader spends half of his day sorting out differences among his team members. In such organizations, the primary responsibility of a team leader is just to solve issues among individuals and motivate them to work together. Remember, the role of a team leader is not just to motivate his team members to adjust with each other and sort out their problems. It is much more.

Female employees appointed for marketing profiles have to move out for client meetings, product demonstrations, presentations and so on. You cannot always call the client to your office. Yes, superiors need to take care of the safety of female colleagues but sometimes it does also affect the overall productivity of the team and eventually organization.

Kiara had to go out of the country for a client meeting. Her family did not approve her travelling alone as they were worried about her safety. Kiara's Organization lost a major account and suffered huge losses.

Male employees are generally preferred over female employees especially in marketing and sales department as they do not have problems moving out or going alone even to the remotest locations. Bosses also have an additional responsibility of taking care of their female employees.

Organizational diversity also sometimes leads to cultural differences leading to stress and frustration among team members. Frustrated employees can never deliver their level best or perform as per the expectations of the seniors. A female employee among all male employees finds it difficult to adjust with them and go out for parties or get - togethers.Male employees also do not feel comfortable with their female counterparts. They are extra careful while interacting with them. Though misbehaving at workplace is absolutely unethical and unacceptable, but if you are extra cautious while dealing with colleagues of opposite gender, you would never be able to enjoy your work. Neither would you feel like coming to work but also avoid participating in activities or taking the initiative of organizing various events or festivals at workplace. Hindu employees show more enthusiasm during Diwali or Holi but when it comes to Christmas, it is just another holiday for them and vice a versa. Nurturing such negative feeling not only spoils the ambience of the workplace but also demotivates employees. Individuals from absolutely different backgrounds find it extremely difficult to adjust and hence the overall productivity of the organization is affected.

- **Role of Communication in Managing Organizational Diversity**

    Communication is indeed an effective tool which plays an important role in binding employees together. Communication plays a crucial role in breaking the ice among employees, bringing them closer to each other and thus managing organizational diversity. An individual may belong to any religion or community, but it is his/her power to communicate which helps him know about his fellow workers. It is essential for individuals to talk and share their experiences. Unless and until, they do so, they would never be able to enjoy their work and treat it as a mere source of burden. Believe me, if employees are asked to work in isolation, they would attend office just for the sake of it.

    In today's scenario of fierce competition, employees need to discuss, brainstorm ideas to reach to innovative solutions which would not only benefit their respective teams but also help their organization to outshine its competitors. Communication in fact helps you to express your ideas and viewpoints. Do not say a "yes" if you feel it is not correct. Remember, freedom of expression is the right of every employee and you just cannot deprive anyone of the same.

    It hardly matters whether the individual is a Christian or a Muslim, has recently joined the organization or is there for quite some time, is an MBA or just a graduate. What is more important is whether he/she is able to do justice to the roles and responsibilities assigned or not? Let individuals come out with their ideas, opinions and also have a say in organization's major decisions.

    One of the most common reasons of misunderstandings and conflicts at the workplace is lack of communication between them and their superiors. Superiors need to communicate with their team members on a regular basis not only to regularly monitor their performance but also motivate them to come out with their best every time. Individuals feel left out and demotivated when their Bosses do not have the time to talk to them. Effective communication enables information to reach all related employees in its desired form. Do not interact with only the top level employees but with every individual associated with organization.

Individuals need to communicate effectively to know about each other's customs, traditions, religions, culture and so on. If you do not allow them to sit together and talk, trust me, they would treat each other as enemies and would find it extremely difficult to work in unison. How would an individual know that the person sitting next to him, who though belongs to a different religion is his fellow worker and is also working for the same motive i.e. to achieve organization's goals and objectives and also for respective career growths? He/she would come to know only when you would allow him/her to communicate effectively with counterparts. Effective communication ensures individuals from varied backgrounds, religions; communities or age groups share a strong rapport and do not face problems working together. Individuals, when effectively communicate seldom fight and solve half of the problems themselves. They escalate the matter to their superiors only when it is really serious and requires their intervention. In a way, effective communication not only manages organizational diversity but also leads to a positive ambience at the workplace. There are situations when some or the other misunderstandings among team members might arise, but it is always better when employees sit face to face, talk and clear the same at the earliest. The productivity is in fact more when employees communicate effectively with each other.

Rising Incidence of Harassment at Workplace and Its Implications for Diversity

The Rising Incidence of Harassment at the Workplace

In recent months, the corporate world across all continents and regions has been impacted by a rising trend of harassment of women at the workplace. The evidence for this can be seen in the almost weekly news and scandals of sexual harassment in the United States and in Asia, which have emerged, as the main centers for these cases. This has grave implications for the practice of organizational diversity and unless, steps are taken to address this growing malaise, the corporate world would soon resemble a jungle where women feel unsafe and harassed and discriminated against. To arrest this trend, business leaders must urgently take steps to restore the confidence of women that their concerns would be taken care of and that their welfare is paramount to the corporates. The point here is that this trend of harassment and discrimination has emerged just when more and more women were entering the corporate world as employees and being promoted to senior positions. The fact that no woman at any level is immune from harassment speaks a sorry tale about the depths to which the corporate world has sunk.

Ways to Check the Dangerous Trend of Harassment: Prevention is Better than Cure

To redress this situation, companies must take all complaints of harassment seriously and investigate them without any bias. The fact that punishment must be meted out to the perpetrators however senior they might be and however up the hierarchy they are. The point here is that a strong message must be sent out to all employees that harassment and discrimination against women would not be tolerated. Apart from this, special committees must be setup to allay the fears of women and to record anonymous complaints from women so that their identities are protected. Further, the women employees must be encouraged to report even the slightest misdemeanors so that the workplace is free of harassment and discrimination of any kind. This means that even the smallest cases of harassment should not be tolerated as these supposedly small incidents if left unpunished would soon morph into serious cases of harassment as the perpetrators feel emboldened to continue their behavior. The key aspect here is that often at the workplace, when it is common for men and women to work together, the line between decency and decorum and boorish behavior is often crossed and once it happens, it would surely assume dangerous proportions. Therefore, it is better to nip such behavior in the bud to prevent it from happening again and to ensure that it does not grow to alarming proportions.

Need for Mindset Change accompanied by Senior Leadership Commitment

Of course, all these steps are meaningless without a corresponding change in mindsets and hence, the mindset of tolerance and acceptance must be inculcated and developed and this must start right from the top. This means that the organizational culture and the DNA must be nurtured and developed in a manner that would produce a corresponding confidence in women and make them feel empowered and enabled. The point here is that often women feel helpless when they are harassed because the perpetrators are either their bosses or those who are in the good books of their superiors. The only way to address this insecurity would be through sending a strong message corresponding with strict action against those who harass and intimidate women. This can only be done if the HR and the diversity teams take a proactive stance against harassment instead of acting on complaints. In other words, by preventing harassment, the organization can fare better than acting on complaints, which means that the damage has already been done. This is the best approach towards harassment and discrimination which when accompanied by a genuine movement towards mindset change would result in a workplace free of harassment and discrimination.

: PART 2 :

CHANGE MANAGEMENT

- **Meaning and Important Concepts**

The business landscape of the 21st century is characterized by rapid change brought about due to technological, economic, political and social changes. It is no longer the case that the managers and employees of firms in this decade can look forward to more of the same every year. In fact, the pace of change is so rapid and the degree of obsolescence if organizations resist change is so brutal that the only way out for many firms is to change or perish. In this context, it becomes critical that organizations develop the capabilities to adapt and steer change in their advantage.

The role of senior managers becomes crucial in driving through change and ensuring that firms are well placed with respect to their competitors. However, it is the case that in many organizations, senior managers actively resist change and in fact thwart change initiatives due to a variety of reasons which would be explored in subsequent sections. This essay examines the barriers to change by senior managers and discusses approaches to mitigate such resistance. The essay begins with a discussion n the role of senior managers as barriers to change and then outlines some approaches on how to get the senior managers on board for change.

It goes without saying that "he who rejects change is the architect of decay and the only human institution that rejects progress is the cemetery." With this axiom in mind, it is critical to understand that unless change is actively embraced, organizations in the 21st century risk obsolescence.

To resist change is as basic as human nature and hence the change managers must adopt an inclusive approach that considers the personality clashes and the ego tussles. It is often the case that in large organizations, there tend to be power centres and fiefdoms and hence the issue of organizational change must address the group dynamics as well as the individual behavioural characteristics.

Only by an understanding of the means by which managers can be brought on board can there be a foundation for suitable approaches. The approaches include a combination of pressure tactics and coordination instead of competition and cooption as well as cooperation. Change agents must realize that wherever possible, they must deal with consensual decision making and if that is not possible, they must walk the talk and be firm in their approach. Managers at all levels have a tendency to resist change and in the high stakes game of change management, it is the ones that can articulate and communicate the change in a clear and coherent manner who succeed.

In conclusion, change is the only constant in business and the landscape of the 21st century is littered with companies that have not adapted to the changing times. Hence, organizations must and should embrace change and the approaches discussed in this paper are part of the solution.

■   **Kinds of Change and the Barriers to Change**

There are different kinds of change that an organization might undertake or be forced to undertake because of internal and external factors. The internal factors for change include reorganization and restructuring to meet the challenges of the future and also to act proactively to initiate change as a means of staying ahead of the competition. The external factors include change that is forced upon the organization because of falling revenues, changing market conditions and the need to adapt to the ever changing business landscape.

Change can be organic which means that it evolves slowly and is like meandering up the gentle slope of a mountain. In this case, the organization and the management have enough time to prepare for change and reorient themselves accordingly. This is the kind of change that is adaptive meaning that firms have the opportunity to adapt themselves to the change.

Change can be radical which is rapid, sudden and uncertain. This is the kind of change that is disruptive and often forces organizations to reorient themselves without adequate notice and warning. It is better for organizations to anticipate change rather than be forced into accepting change that is rapid and sudden.

We have seen how managers at different levels resist change and how this resistance manifests itself. Apart from the ideological and personality issues, there is the very real possibility of change being resisted because the "visibility" of what comes next is not clear. For instance, many managers tend to resist change because the change initiators have not clearly spelt out the outcomes of the changes and the possible impacts that such changes have on the organization. This is the realm of the "known unknowns" and the "unknown unknowns" which arise because of ambiguity, complexity and uncertainty. Hence, the resistance to change can come about due to the lack of coherence in the vision and mission and because the change is not clearly communicated as well.

Finally, the rapidity with which change is introduced can upset the organization structures that are usually rigid and bureaucratic with bean counters at all levels resisting and actively thwarting change. Hence, it needs to be remembered that change initiators take into account all these factors when introducing changes. The possible approaches in dealing with these resistances would be discussed in the next section.

- **Overcoming Barriers to Change**

Research has shown that the best way to get the senior managers at all levels interested in the change initiatives is by engaging them and seeking their buy-in for the change management process. Studies have proved that the managers in the upper echelons buy into the change from a strategic perspective where the accent is on performance and hence radical or disruptive change is seen as part and parcel of an organizations development. Managers at the middle level can be made to see the value inherent in change and hence they can be brought on board. The frontline managers' views and inputs can be sought and thereby their cooperation and participation in the change obtained. These are the broad outlines and the following detailed sets of approaches can be pursued as well.

Make Them the Hero

By making the managers the change drivers and change initiators is often the best way of securing their buy-in. The point here is that by getting the managers to be the ones who are implementing change and by giving them centre stage, it is possible to secure their participation.

By definition, senior managers are highly capable, motivated and ambitious. By making them the stars of the change process, their innate abilities can be harnessed to the benefit of the organization. It is often better to have a close association with the senior managers to achieve the desired results.

Show them the potential of Change

By selling change and the value of such change to the organizations and themselves the senior managers can be persuaded to accept change. The point to note is that senior managers must be told what their role in the post change scenario would be and by making them see themselves in the future vision, they can be made to play a key part in the change management. As has been mentioned earlier, if the benefits of the change are explained and by persuading that the change does not involve downsizing or other reduction in roles and responsibilities, the senior managers can be expected to be partners rather than resisters in the change management process.

Painting the Alternatives

This is the stick part of the carrot and stick approach wherein senior managers are told of the urgent need for change and by indicating to them what the consequences for themselves and the organization would be if the change does not succeed. By painting harsh alternative scenarios like declining market share and repercussions of layoffs and downsizing if the change does not succeed would make the senior managers realize the flip side of resistance. In this way, they can be persuaded to accept the business realities behind the change process.

Involving Them in the Change

By adopting a "hands on" approach that would involve "all hands" and including all the stakeholders, senior managers can be brought on board. The point is that by adopting an inclusive approach and giving a sense of ownership to the senior managers and taking their inputs and feedback would ensure that the key aspect of "engagement" is achieved. As has been pointed out throughout this paper, the key to senior manager participation in the change initiatives is through engagement and only by communicating clearly the benefits of change and by positing the alternatives would it be possible to engage with senior managers. A suitable narrative of the changes and the impact that they have on the senior managers must be communicated to all levels and there must be a process in place to bring on board as many managers as possible. Personality clashes and power politics can be addressed by consensual approaches to decision making and by adopting a carrot and stick approach as described above.

- **The Role of Senior Managers as Barriers to Change**

It is often the case that when change programs are initiated in firms, there is a level of resistance from senior managers due to a number of reasons. These range from protecting their turfs to uncertainties regarding their position after the change is implemented and to ego clashes as well as power politics. The ways in which they can manifest their resistance to change ranges from citing time pressures and constraints involved in implementing the change, citing operational pressures in bureaucratic and mechanistic organizations where the rigid structure does not lend itself to change and finally, by pointing out earlier instances of change that have failed. The point to note is that it is human nature to be comfortable with the status quo and hence barriers to organizational change are psychological more than anything else.

In the case of senior managers, the barriers to change arise because they would want to protect their turfs, resist change because it has been initiated by a rival power group and finally, there is a tendency to resist change because the senior managers do not see a role for them after the change is implemented.

It needs to be remembered that while bad strategies result in failed change initiatives, good strategies without proper execution and implementation lead to the same result. Hence, it is not enough to have a good strategy in place if there is no viable means of execution and implementation.

When we discuss about the barriers of change from senior managers, we need to distinguish between the levels of managers. This is necessary as the barrier to change is different at each level. For instance, the front line managers often resist change because they fear for their positions post change. Since these managers are vulnerable to the changes wrought by technology where their positions become obsolete because of automation, the front line managers tend to resist change because of this aspect. The front line managers might also be disinterested in the change if it does not impact the day to day workings or the operational issues. This is the case of the "distance" between the change initiators and the operational managers that can result in the change being remote and the front line managers being unconcerned with the change.

The middle level managers who form the "sandwich" between the workforce and senior management have a pivotal role to play in change management initiatives as they are the ones who communicate the changes to the workforce and in turn have to report on the success or otherwise of the initiatives to the senior management. These middle tier managers often resist change because of inertia and a status quo mentality which makes them impervious to new realities. It is a fact that the middle tier managers in bureaucratic or machine structure organizations have a lot from continuing with the status quo because of the tangible and intangible benefits that accrue to them.

Finally, and most importantly, the managers in the upper echelons tend to resist change because they have personal fiefdoms that they protect jealously. Further, they have big personalities because of which the possibilities of ego clashes among the top management are very real. In cases where the change is initiated by one faction, the rival faction tends to oppose such change purely on personality issues alone. It is also noteworthy that senior managers and managers at all levels exhibit tendencies that are described in theory as value enhancing or utility maximizing (the so-called "agency problems") which would make them behave in ways contrary to the interests of the shareholders. These are some of the characterizations of the levels of managers and their tendencies to resist change.

- **Global Financial Crisis and Organizational Change**

Resistance to change is inevitable as there are many parties who stand to lose from change and apart from the status quoists there are vested interests who would oppose change. The changes that the organizations and the companies introduced in the wake of the global financial crisis were systemic and fundamental in nature and hence there would be many reasons for people and employees in these organizations to resist change. The primary reason why the people would resist change is that because of job losses and the associated risks of layoffs and restricting, they stand to lose and hence there is a strong element of resistance that enters the discussion.

Since the organizations in Australia undertook drastic changes to the way they worked, the people working in these organizations have every reason to resist the changes because they are at the losing end of the changes and hence have a stake in resisting change. This goes for the majority of people who were affected by the downturn and whose jobs and careers were at stake because of the global financial crisis.

The other reason for people or organizations to resist change is that the global financial crisis was systemic in nature and hence called for fundamental changes in which the system operated. This meant that the people or organizations at the receiving end of these changes had to bear very drastic changes in the way they operated and hence those who gain by following the status quo had every reason to resist the change. This was especially the case with organizations that underwent restricting and cost cutting where though there were no drastic job losses, many of the perks and benefits for the employees were cut leading to widespread dissatisfaction and discontent with the kind of changes that were being proposed. Hence, this is the second most important reason for people or organizations to resist changes in the wake of the downturn caused by the global financial crisis.

The third reason why organizations resisted the changes in the aftermath of the global financial crisis is that many of the changes introduced led to regulatory and legal changes in the way organizations operated and hence there was every chance that these organizations had to implement rules and regulations that would curb excessive risk taking and speculation. Given the enormous benefits that these methods of risk taking and speculation bring to the people and organizations concerned, it is indeed the case that they would not be willing to forego these benefits. Hence, this is a very important reason for people and organizations to resist the changes introduced in the aftermath of the global financial crisis.

In conclusion, change is something that is constant but given the inherent tendency of the bureaucratic structures in organizations to resist change, there is always an element of resistance to change. Particularly when the changes are drastic as seen in the case of the global financial crisis, there tends to be steadfast opposition to change by the organizations and hence this is a fact of life that the change makers and the change agents have to factor in their strategies.

- **Why Some Organizations are Better at Driving Change ?**

We live in a world where increasing complexity is the order of the day and the business landscape is characterized by a rapid turnover of companies which find themselves dethroned from their position because of outmoded thinking or anachronistic strategies.

For instance, Nokia and RIM (the maker of Blackberry) were at the top of the leading mobile companies a couple of years ago. Now, their places have been taken by Apple and Samsung because both Nokia and RIM got bogged down due to a combination of internal problems as well as the failure to spot changing trends. They could not foresee the trends which indicated that mobile phones would be used for purposes very much different from making and receiving calls and instead they would be used in ways that would revolutionize the concept of mobiles as one-stop solutions for a wide variety of consumer needs. In other words, these companies were victims of complexity.

To deal with complexity and uncertainty, companies need to shift the lens with which they are viewing the business landscape and hence change according to the situation rather than have long term strategies based on fixed notions or projections that become obsolete within months. Change management in these cases becomes critical and not just necessary or essential. And to adapt to change, there needs to be a mindset and attitude change rather than plain business strategies. The mindset change is something that needs the top management to actively involve themselves in "winning the hearts and minds" of the employees and the other stakeholders. Only when there is a "buy-in" from the employees to the change initiatives being undertaken by the management can they succeed.

The example of the legendary founder of Apple, the Late Steve Jobs is an excellent case in point as to how charismatic CEO's can go about "winning the hearts and minds" of employees. Jobs was not only instrumental in turning around Apple Inc. from near bankruptcy to a leader in the industry, but also ushered in a paradigm shift as to the way in which the computing and software industry operated. Another example is the case of Google which has made the organization of information its business and has ensured that the way in which we function everyday has been transformed. In both cases, the CEO's could inspire and motivate their employees to believe in their vision and by dint of hard work and diligent attention to detail, they succeeded in being "change agents".

These examples show how change can be initiated in response to ever changing and complex scenarios that business leaders face. What are needed are a compelling vision and a fresh way of looking at issues. Once the vision is articulated, there needs to be a push to reframe the issues and look at problems in a new light. Making sense of complexity becomes easier if the strategies are rethought according to changing circumstances. In conclusion, we need not succumb to complexity and instead use it to drive change that is lasting and beneficial to the company.

- **Role of Catalysts in Organizational Change**

The other one in this series on Change Management have listed the business imperatives for change as well as the various barriers to change that arise from internal and external resisters. In this, we examine the other side of driving change and that is to do with the role of people who can act as catalysts in driving change.

Every organization has high performers and those who are steady as well as those who make up the bottom of the performance chart. Though it is not necessarily the case that the top performers are the ones who should drive change, more often than not, that is the case. However, there might be pearls waiting to be discovered as well.

The broader point that we are making is that management and the HR department must institute a program that would identify potential "change agents" who can act as catalysts for the change initiatives which the management might be planning.

Most organizations have lists of employees whom they consider "High Potentials" or "Fast Trackers" which indicate that the people in these lists are being marked for higher positions and they are groomed accordingly. In addition to that, the management along with the HR department can compile a list of people who take initiative in their roles and are not content with merely doing their assigned tasks but are proactive about trying on new ideas and concepts. These people are an asset to any organization and the management must identify such people and get them together to brainstorm about new initiatives and how to make the organization more successful.

The qualities that are needed in such change catalysts are impatience with the status quo, out of the box thinking, a different perspective than others about the strategies that the company is pursuing etc. When we mentioned that such people might not be necessarily the top performers, what we meant is that there might be employees at all levels who given the chance to change the existing paradigm may very well end up as the stars that the company needs. And when there is a need for change, such people turn out to assets that the company had undervalued all the while.

The point about the catalysts for change initiatives is that they have the personal attributes needed to motivate and inspire others to follow their lead. The key point here is that they would be people enablers and leaders as far as leading from the front are concerned. Plus, they would with their infectious attitude towards change be able to convince those who are skeptical about the change initiatives. Hence, organizations need to rethink their system of rating the employees and include the change agent part of it and maybe, assign it more weight in determining the overall grade of the employee. Though this does not take anything away from the employees who are diligent and produce results, change initiatives can be driven only by a new way of thinking and hence non-linear thinking must be encouraged.

Creating Sustainable Change - How to create and sustain change ?

Who doesn't like change and who doesn't want to change? These are certainly truisms in the 21st century landscape where businesses proclaim their commitment to change and exhort their employees to "Be the change you want to see". However, having a vision and mission statement that commits to change is different from actualizing the change. There are numerous examples of so-called "paradigm shifters" who have flattered to deceive. The best known example of this is the launch of Hotmail as the world's first free web based mail service.

There was lot of hype surrounding Hotmail and its legendary founder, Sabeer Bhatia, became an icon of sorts. Now, a decade later, how many teenagers who have entered the cyber world in the last few years even know about Hotmail? So, the point here is that having a great idea is just the first step. And executing it to actually creating a shift in the way things are done is the next step. Companies often do step 1 and step 2 pretty well. You might very well ask what the problem is.

The problem is the sustainability aspect of change. Or, put another way: How to create and sustain change by not losing the momentum? This is the challenge that companies face in the contemporary world where your last performance matters more than anything else. So, investors and the general public eagerly await the new product launches and the "Next Big Thing" from Microsoft, Google or Facebook and are disappointed if the offering does not live up to their expectations. It is no longer the case that companies can ride on their reputations created over a legacy system. Now, they have to constantly innovate and do better or even do best each time they go to the market. With the ever shortening product cycle and the dwindling time to market period, companies are literally engaged in a "race to the bottom" as far as their competitors are concerned.

So, how does one sustain the momentum? The first thing to do is to create an atmosphere in the company or make the organizational culture "Change oriented" which makes automatic the process of listening to the market and responding appropriately. Next, invest in people who can be "change agents" and then make all efforts to retain them and nourish them. Creation of an organizational culture and nurturing change agents go hand in hand. The final step is to incorporate change into the organizational DNA so that change becomes a constant in the way the company does business. Taken together these steps represent the maintaining of the change process and building on the momentum created by the initial burst towards change. It needs to be remembered that sustainability is important not only from the environmental perspective but also from the organizational commitment to change. In conclusion, the "change game" ought to be practiced by companies if they are to remain abreast of the latest trends and to make the marketplace their own.

- **Top-Down versus Bottom-Up Change**

It is often the case that companies are faced with a dilemma about whether the change initiatives must be driven from the top or they should be organic from the bottom up. This is especially the case with organizations that are growing in size where the increase employee base or the skyrocketing sales and revenues mean that the top management's scope of control is more and hence driving change from the top alone might not just work. And for those organizations that initiate change from the top, they might find themselves in a situation where the middle and bottom layers of the organizational hierarchy may not be responsive or energized in the way the top managements wants them to be. So, the existential questions as to whether there ought to a spontaneous involvement from all the levels, or whether the top management must induce the change, are very real and need to be answered for change initiatives to succeed.

The answer as to which option is preferable depends on a number of factors. First, any change initiative would succeed only if it is communicated appropriately and to all levels. Honest, transparency and feedback loops must be the elements of the change initiative. Next, the employees ought to have a voice in the way the change initiative is managed. For a change initiative to be successful the top management has to communicate and the employees have to respond. Like Bees gathering around honey and being driven by the Queen Bee, organizations have to ensure that while the CEO or the other top managers initiate the change, employees at all levels must take to the change as well. So, a mix of having the top management initiate the change and letting the employees take over from them works best for larger organizations where micro management by the top management might not work.

Examples of organizations that have embraced change successfully include 3M, Google and Facebook where the visionary leaders at the top ensured that the initial germ of an idea was seeded in the employees and then they let the trees grow by sampling nourishing them from time to time while at the same time preferring organic growth rather than transplanted growth. The other extreme is marked by failures like HP where the top management was unable to make their employees buy into their change strategies. Of course, this is not to say that organizations need visionary leaders as essential elements of success. Though it helps, companies can make do with success if they have a combination of people enablers who take pride in their organizations and can empower the employees to participate in the change initiatives.

In conclusion, change can be driven solely from the top. However, for continued success, change has to come from within each employee and this can only happen in organizations that have an organizational culture that encourages each employee to contribute to the initiatives. Change can thrive where there is an institutional catalyst and hence the key takeaway is that the organizational structures have to be built in such a way that no one individual can either make or mar the chances of success.

- **Role of HR in Change Management**

  This module has covered the various aspects of change management and the roles played by senior management as well as the CEO in top down change and the role of employees at all levels in bottom up change. The role played by "support functions" in an organization in facilitating change. Specifically, it looks at the role that the Human Resources Department can play in supporting and enabling change. Before we launch into the specifics of how the HR can facilitate change, it needs to be remembered that change management is first and foremost about people and their capacity to adapt to change. Since, the HR department is all about recruiting, training and monitoring employee performance; it has a key role to play in any change management program. There are different aspects in which HR can play a significant role and we shall consider some of them.

  The HR department has to ensure that employees are motivated to undertake the change and participate in the change management program. For this to happen, they need to recruit the right people who can think out of the box and can bring a fresh perspective to the table.

  Companies like Yahoo and Intel look for people who can think non-linearly and in unconventional ways. Once the right people are recruited, they need to be encouraged and mentored so that they act as "change agents". This is the key element of a successful change management strategy and this is where the HR department has a stellar role to play. Many companies have a separate role for a "People

Manager" wherein he or she has the responsibility of mentoring and nurturing talent. Some examples are Fidelity and IBM that have designated people managers who are apart from the line managers and so their primary duty is to ensure the enabling and empowering of employees who report to them in a dotted line fashion.

The point here is that the HR department must be encouraged to look for people who can act as catalysts for change and who can motivate other employees to participate in the change initiative. Since the HR department is staffed by people who have degrees in organizational and personal behavior, enlisting their help in driving change is a crucial element in the overall change management strategy. Great companies have great leaders and great leaders are "enabled" and "energized" by highly supportive environments that nurture and reward talent. The last aspect of reward and recognition is the final element in a successful change management plan and if the employees who enthusiastically participate in change initiatives are suitably rewarded and adequately recognized, there is an added incentive for them to further the change initiative.

In conclusion, HR needs to be seen as much more than a supporting function and instead, must be viewed as integral to the organization's change management strategy. Companies like the TATA group and Infosys are highly successful at change management because their personnel policies are employee friendly and are geared towards getting the best out of their employees.

- **Role of Innovation in Change Management**

We have seen how various factors contribute to the propagation of change within an organization. For instance, change can be catalyzed through change agents and can be driven from the top as well as from the bottom. In this point, we will look at the crucial role of innovation in driving change. For quite some time now, it has been known that companies need to innovate constantly if they are to stay ahead of the pack in terms of competitiveness.

Innovation can take many forms and some of them are discontinuous innovation, continuous innovation and dynamically continuous innovation. We shall discuss what each mean in the next paragraph. Suffice to say that unless companies innovate they cannot move up the value chain and unless they move up the value chain, they cannot remain competitive. So, to make changes to the organizational processes and its strategy, companies need to innovate constantly.

Innovation can produce sudden and dramatic changes to the way business is done and the way consumers experience changes to the products and services made by the companies.

This is the discontinuous innovation which is sudden and has a huge impact on the way the company goes about its business. On the other hand, innovation can be gradual and incremental which is the continuous innovation way which means that the company introduces refinements to its products so that consumers adjust and adapt in steps. Finally, there is the dynamically continuous innovation which affects the way in which the company adapts to changing market conditions and changes in consumer behavior trends to make a positive impact on the consumer psyche.

The point here is that no matter what kind of innovation the company adopts, the prerequisite for change management is innovation and without innovation, a company cannot expect its internal and external environment to be to its advantage. For instance, if Apple comes out with its new iPhone and disrupts the way in which consumers perceive a phone, it is discontinuous innovation. If Apple modifies its iPhone in a dynamic manner according to the changing customer preferences, it is dynamically continuous innovation. If it releases its iPhone after minor tweaks, then it is continuous innovation. For Apple to make a mark in the customer experience, it has to keep changing continuously and hence has to innovate constantly to keep abreast of the consumer trends and the competition.

An example of a company that constantly strives to be the best when it concerns change and innovation is 3M Corporation. This company is known for its world class innovation teams which drive change throughout the company and keep its consumers happy and its competitors on their toes. The way in which 3M drives innovation to produce change is indeed exemplary and worthy of emulation. Hence, innovation should be the mantra for companies wishing to change their internal environments and in the process change the way they project themselves in the external marketplace.

In conclusion, we are living in times where the rapid turnover of ideas and products in the marketplace has reached a stage where it is no longer enough to be best in the class. Instead, the pursuit of excellence and the search for excellence are the hallmarks of a truly successful and world class company and hence all companies must undertake efforts to drive innovation and change within and without.

Are External Consultants Needed for Change Management Programs to Succeed ?

Many organizations take the help of external consultants in identifying, recommending and implementing change. This looks at whether there is indeed a case to be made for external consultants to help with the change management programs.

If we look at the reasons why organizations rope in external consultants like McKinsey, BCG and Booze Allen group (among others) we find that they do so mainly because they need an independent and objective perspective on what needs to be changed and how it should be achieved.

For instance, companies like Jaguar, BP and Shell have all relied on external consultants to help them with their change management programs. And, they have been relatively successful in their efforts as can be seen in the way they have transformed themselves in the marketplace.

However, there have been notable failures as well. For instance, the Parry's group failed spectacularly in its efforts to change its business processes and outlook towards the market. Despite taking the help of external consultants, the company could not transform itself. So, what is that differentiates whether external consultants succeed or fail to help companies in their change management programs. First, there needs to be cooperation with the consultant from the entire top management and not merely the CEO or a few directors/managers. The point is that the external consultants must not fall prey to the office politics and hence the entire leadership must stand solidly behind them.

Next, there cannot be any information that is withheld from the external consultants. The key to change is that complete information about the organization and its strengths and most importantly, its flaws must be visible and so the external consultants must have the full cooperation of the people who are responsible for implementing their recommendations. In fact, one of the reasons the CEO or the Board of Directors often take the help of consultants is that they need an objective view of the situation which is unbiased and not tinted by the prejudiced perspective of politicking employees.

The other aspect that makes organizations rely on external consultants is because these consultants have experience in dealing with companies in similar industries and hence can apply their expertise and experience to recommend specific changes. However, it is the case that consultants can get too close to the management to the point where they are compromised because of their proximity to the powers that be. Some examples of this include the Arthur Anderson and Enron saga where both the consultants (Anderson Consulting) and Enron became partners in swindling the employees and the people. Closer home, the way in which PWC or Price Waterhouse Coopers was a partner to the Satyam scandal shows that there are downsides to having consultants guide the companies.

In conclusion, consultants bring a fresh perspective to dealing with organizational issues and hence are vital to the change management program. However, there is a need to observe professional rules of conduct and there must be ethical behavior from both sides of the equation.

- **Why Change Management Programs Often Fail ? Some Ways to Actualize Change**

We have heard the story several times. A large conglomerate wants to implement a change management program, which it then announces amidst much fanfare and hype. The top leadership waxes eloquent on the need to change and why the organization must actualize change. However, a few years down the line, things are still bad for the company and the change program has bitten the dust. What are the reasons for this? First, there is something called "change fatigue" that sets in when the change being instituted is part of a long string of change management programs that have been going on in the organization. Second, the resistance to change (a topic we discussed at length in previous s) is the next reason. Third, the employees might have little faith in the top management and the confidence in the management team is at such a situation that the employees do not take anything that the management says seriously.

Therefore, the obvious question is what the management should do to actualize change. First, create an engaged organization where the buy-in for the change is secured deep and wide within the organizational hierarchy. This means that the "Sandwich Layer" of middle management and the key power centers in the organizations are on the same page as the management.

Second, have execution clarity, which means that the top management knows what it wants and how it should go about actualizing change. The message of change must be lucid and coherent and the senior as well as the other layers of management must think through the change process. Third, create a critical mass of "enabled leaders" who would carry through the change and who know what exactly the change entails and how to go about it.

Fourth, the senior management must realize that "in unity lies strength" and hence, must build a cohesive organizational culture that does not fray at the edges or is hollow in the middle. In other words, there needs to be a sense of purpose about the change process and how it must be actualized by all levels of management. Fifth and finally, the Project Management Office and the Governance structures responsible for change must articulate, implement, seek feedback, and close out the change process as well as plug any leakages. The important point to note here is that the PMO must be vested with full powers to implement the change and as happens with economies and politics, governance mechanisms in organizations must not be clogged. In other words, the organizational arteries must be clear and free from appendages. If these elements of the change management process are taken into account, actualizing the change would be relatively easy.

Finally, the whole point of the change program must be to engage with the employees at all levels and ensure that the change management program targets the core of the organizations competencies and vision and mission. In conclusion, change management programs can only succeed when these elements are conjoined together to create a coherent and understandable narrative that the employees can relate to.

- **Middle Level Management - Sandwich Layer and its Importance to Organizations**

In previous s, at many places, we have discussed how the middle management is in the unique position of actualizing change in organizations. We have talked about how the middle management needs to be brought on board for any meaningful change and how the senior leadership cannot alone get things going in any organization. The reason for the importance of the middle management is that they are the "sandwich" layer or the layer between the top management and the employees or the "boots on the ground". In other words, the middle management is in the unique position of being placed in such a way that they have access to the top management and they can command the loyalty of the regular member's employees. Hence, any organizational initiative has to necessarily take into account the importance of the middle management in the larger scheme of things.

Many organizational change initiatives fail because the top management would not have communicated the change imperative and the steps to be taken to actualize them to the middle management in a coherent manner. Moreover, the middle management would not have been brought on board or their cooperation and buy-in secured.

Hence, the primary imperative for any policy to be effective is that the managers must be driven to implement the same without leakage and friction. This is the reason many organizations conduct "offsite workshops" for the middle managers where they are explicitly told on what to do and how to implement the change. Further, the sandwich layer means that they can get feedback from the ground and pass it on to the top management. In this way, they act as the bridge between the top management and the employees on the ground.

The middle management is usually the layer that has the highest stakes in ensuring compliance with organizational policies. Appraisals and reviews are conducted by them and the bonus and the salary hikes are decided by them in consultation with senior management. Often, it is the case that the quantum of bonus or the salary hike for the regular member's employees is decided based on the recommendation of the manager. Hence, the middle managers have to make sure that the employees are conforming to organizational policies as well as ensure that the senior management is made aware of the feedback from the employees. In this way, the middle management acts as conduit between the top and the bottom.

Of course, in many organizations, the middle managers are often played by the power centers and the vested interests because of intra-organizational politics. While not condemning this outright as this is inevitable in all organizations, the point needs to be made that the CEO and the executive leadership must keep a tab on such power plays and ensure that the organization does not suffer. The point here is that the middle management is often at the receiving end from both sides and hence, they are vital and at the same time, an often neglected factor in organizational success.

- **Bureaucracy and Organizational Change**

The very word bureaucracy conjures images of sloth, inefficiency and status quoist mindset. To associate bureaucracy with change would thus be looked as an oxymoron. However, it is the case that some large organizations that were otherwise bureaucratic in their organizational structures managed to bring about change in the way they worked. The best known example of this is the exemplary leadership provided by Lee Iacocca in his time at Ford and Chrysler, the auto majors in the United States. For the current generation, Lee Iacocca might be relatively unknown. But, for those who remember his extraordinary contributions to these organizations are aware of the way in which he turned them around in the face of stiff opposition from the bureaucracy. The book, Iacocca (an autobiography written by him) is a must read for those who want to implement change in large organizations.

If we look at the cases of large organizations where change did not succeed, we need not look farther than the governmental bureaucracies in all countries (especially India) where change is the farthest thing in the minds of the bureaucrats.

To give an example of a private sector organization that could not drive through change because of bureaucracy, we find General Motors and HP among the leading contenders. In both cases, the entrenched mindset which resisted any kind of change stymied the efforts of the leadership as well as those who wanted to bring about reform in these organizations.

So, what is it that makes some organizations better able to reform their bureaucracies and others fail to do so? For starters, the organizational structure is the key to implementing change management and the way in which it is designed is often the differentiating factor between success and failure. The arteries of the bureaucratic organizations tend to get clogged with time leading to institutional resistance to change; next, the way in which the business imperatives are defined is crucial to making the employees buy into the change initiative. For instance, if the employees feel that change is being driven because of the personalities of the leaders and not necessarily because of the need to make more profits or respond to competition better is a major put off when change initiatives are launched.

So, the bottom line is that the structure as well as the people making up of the parts of the organization needs to be changed first if lasting and permanent change is to be achieved in the organization. Finally, the way in which change is communicated internally to the employees makes a lot of difference in the way the change program is implemented and determines the success or otherwise of the initiative. The top leadership must be honest and truthful in their communication to the employees as far as telling them about the business drivers for change. In most cases, top leadership talks about change as though it is their pet project driven solely by ego and personal interests. Only when employees believe that the change program is needed because of valid and relevant business factors can there be an acceptance and buy in of the initiative.

Change Management in Family owned Businesses versus Professionally run Companies

Is it easier to drive through change in family owned businesses or professionally run companies ? This is a question that is uppermost on most management experts' minds as change in any organization is hard to achieve and if there are barriers that are institutional or structural then it becomes harder to drive through change. For instance, many family-owned businesses like the TATA and the Reliance Group often have charismatic and visionary leaders who are drawn from the family that has a controlling stake.

On the other hand, professionally managed companies like Unilever and P&G are run by managers who need to answer all the stakeholders apart from those who have a majority stake in the company. So, the point is that it is easier for a leader who has to answer to fewer stakeholders to drive through change as opposed to a manager who has to take into account the needs of many stakeholders.

This is the reason that Reliance has been hugely successful in implementing visionary and unique change programs over the course of the last few decades whereas other companies have had moderate successes in driving through organizational change. Of course, Infosys is the exception as the company runs on an owner-manager basis where the major stakeholders run the company professionally instead of like family business manner. This accounts for the phenomenal growth of the company over the years where its visionary leaders were able to carry all the stakeholders with their business acumen and entrepreneurial spirit. On the other hand, companies like Unilever and P&G often take their time to drive organizational change because of lack of commitment from the managerial class or due to the absence of a motivational leader who holds a stake as well.

The point here is that when the combination of a visionary leader with substantial stake arises, and then there is the double whammy of vision and votes on the board which make it easier for the organization to drive through change. Of course, the flip side is that the change program might fail because it is not well rounded or comprehensive and just relies solely on the leaders' abilities. On the other hand, it is common to find companies like Unilever and P&G institute organizational change that is lasting and comprehensive mainly because of the various levels the change management program goes through before acceptance.

It is clear that for effective change to be institutionalized, the change management program must have a blend of vision and nuts and bolts depth which comes if the leader can also succeed in getting the change program vetted by all the stakeholders. Hence, companies like Infosys and to a certain extent the TATA group have managed to drive through change that is both cutting edge and has sufficient depth. However, this is not to say that either family businesses or professionally run companies have a grip over change management. Just that in the case of the former, it is easier to get buy in whereas in the case of the latter, the change management program has to go through several layers of approval.

In conclusion, companies that have visionaries who can carry large sections of the organization along with them often succeed in driving through change better than companies that are bureaucratic or whose organizational arteries have become clogged due to inertia and slowness to adapt to the marketplace.

■   **Change is the only Constant in the 21st Century**

The business landscape of the 21st century is characterized by ever changing trends and events that happen with so much rapidity that they take most business leaders by surprise. Considering the high turnover of ideas and fads, it is no wonder that companies' and their offerings in terms of products and services fail to click in the marketplace more often than not. Given this background it is not surprising that business leaders often throw up their hands in despair at this flux and uncertainty that affects the way their companies operate. Hence, it would be fair to say that the only constant in this century is change and companies and the leaders who lead them should be prepared to deal with change that is rapid and sudden at the same time.

We have discussed how innovation can take several forms ranging from slow and gradual improvements to sudden and discontinuous change. The bottom line for many companies is that they have to innovate to just stay ahead of the competition and it is no longer enough or sufficient to roll out a product a year or an improved version every now and then.

Such is the pace of change that companies like Apple and Google often release products and version along with software every few months so that customers are always a click away from the latest version. Given this high rate of change, it is not surprising that the legendary Bill Gates of Microsoft himself is unable to keep up with the torrent of new products and services that dominate the software landscape. Indeed, it is ironical that Bill Gates who is the author of the bestselling "Business at the Speed of Thought" is somewhat anachronistic in this hyper speed age.

On the other hand, the future belongs to people like Mark Zuckerberg of Facebook who comes up with innovative and market shattering ideas so often that most commentators wonder about how he and his team can do it so often. It has been said that companies need to change internally and externally with such agility that the name of the game is change. And this is what Facebook does with its approach towards new product launches that surprise the stock markets and impress the users. Another company that has made a habit of constantly changing and keeping ahead of the competition is Intel which has so far managed to remain as a leader in its own right despite being around for a long time and in spite of its size.

The point here is that the Millennial Generation measures time by the nanoseconds and hence, they are in constant need of new products and services. And this is something that marketers and companies ought to recognize when they devise products and services for this generation. That is precisely what the companies mentioned above have been doing. Considering the shift in emphasis away from manufacturing towards services and application development as opposed to basic product development world over, it is time for companies to realize that the need for innovation and the speed at which they innovate remain the critical success factors to succeed in the marketplace of the 21st century. In conclusion, it is no longer the case that companies work 12 hours a day to keep up with the competition. Instead, those companies that can leverage the 24/7 culture and embrace the change wave would succeed.

- **What is Strategic Change ? - Meaning and its Theories**
  What is Strategic Change ?

In response to the fast changing and fluid marketplace and industry landscapes, many management thinkers came with theories of strategic change. The first among them was the legendary Peter Drucker who coined the term Age of Discontinuity to describe the way in which disruptive change affects us.

In Drucker's model, the four sources of discontinuity are globalization, cultural pluralism, knowledge capital, and new technologies. The main idea behind this theory is that extrapolating into the future by using the existing models is ineffective as the rapidity with which change was barreling down on corporations made all models redundant within no time. Instead, what Drucker proposed was that firms explore the drivers of change and strategize according to which aspect was most likely to affect the firm in the future.

Future Shock

Another management thinker, Alvin Toffler, came up with an idea about the intersection of different paradigms and the accelerating rates of change and their impact on businesses. He used the term Future Shock to describe how the changes in technology, move towards globalism, resource constraints, and finally, the shortening of time itself were akin to the future arriving even before one could prepare for it and hence he likened human civilization being shocked by the future.

In recent years, Malcolm Gladwell, used the term Tipping Points, to describe the phenomenon of trends acquiring critical mass and then taking off to impact business and society in the process. In addition, Gary Hamel postulated the concept of Strategic Decay to explain how the value of each strategy decays over time irrespective of how brilliant the strategy was in the first place. What these thinkers were attempting is to explain how change is the only constant and hence, businesses ought to be prepared for anything to happen and hence must strategize and build their business models accordingly.

Strategic Change in the Real World

After the discussion on the theorists and their ideas, it is time to consider how strategic change is actualized in the real world. The example of Nokia which was one of the leading makers of the mobile handsets till a few years ago and which now finds itself at the bottom of the heap along with Blackberry reminds us that the strategic drift occurs without anyone noticing it and by the time it is noticed, it is too late. On the other hand, the collapse of once famous companies like Chrysler point to the transformational change that is sudden and radical in nature.

The key aspect about strategic change is that it is difficult to predict and control. Hence, the optimal way to deal with it is to expect the unexpected and be ready for anything. Unless companies embrace change, they are likely to be fossilized and unless companies prepare to deal with sudden, unpredictable, discontinuous, and radical change, they are likely to go the way of the dinosaurs. Finally, many companies proclaim that they are changing whereas it is superficial and the world comes to know later on that their change models were neither broad nor deep.

- **Change Management: Why the First 100 Days Targets are a Myth ?**

How often we hear of business leaders and CEO's who have just taken over proclaim that they would undertake radical change in the first 100 days? How often do we also hear politicians and other personalities promising the moon within the first 100 days? Of course, we don't get to know how many of these changes have transpired in reality since by the time the first 100 days are over, we would have moved on to other matters.

The point here is that in this 24/7 culture of constant change, the temptation to set ambitious targets to achieve the goals within a short time is indeed something that even the most realistic of leaders cannot resist. However, there is a certain limit to which such announcements and agendas for change can be actualized as real world problems, be it in business or governance, are hardly going to be solved within short periods.

The misconceptions surrounding the first 100 days achievements for change and realization of goals should be rightly called so as it is often difficult to actualize change within such a short period of time.

For instance, it takes time to build a team that would be in consonance with the CEO's vision and mission. Often, building a team with those who are comfortable with the CEO and vice versa takes time. Next, the on the job performance of any CEO cannot be measured within the first 100 days as the lingering issues from the past leaders or the previous CEO would continue to cast a shadow over the CEO's performance. Though in politics, it is easy to blame the previous dispensation, it is not often the case that we hear CEO's blaming the previous management since there is certain continuity in the business world in the transition process.

The other aspect or the myth is that CEO's can get down to business the moment they take over. It takes months and even years of patient effort for the fruits to ripen and show results and hence, new CEO's often have to prove their mettle. This means that they need to have an extended run in their position for them to actualize change.

The reason for the 100 days myth is that business leaders like politicians have a "honeymoon" period once they take over where their employees and constituents are willing to tolerate them during this time and hence, give them a breather before they become demanding. Therefore, it is often tempting for the business leaders to set ambitious targets for the first 100 days. Without discounting the importance of this imperative, it needs to be mentioned that having unrealistic expectations from the new CEO would be self-defeating.

Finally, change is glacial and the profound slowness with which change is actualized means that there has to be a mutual communication between the CEO and the employees that is grounded in base expectations and is contextual in nature. Only then would the floors of the company not be littered with the broken glass from the ceilings of euphoria and hyperbole.

Between Two Paradigms: The Changing Role of Management
From the Smokestack Era to the Digital Era

The role of management has changed over the decades as the paradigm shift from manufacturing to services and then to the emerging view of organizations as a holistic whole interacting with its environment in a symbiotic manner. This paradigm shift has engineered and engendered a corresponding shift in the management thought and practice. For instance, it is now common for management experts to stress on the organization and its interaction with its environment as opposed to a machine like organization that is standalone and functions on its own. It has also changed the importance given to employees who are now treated as key sources of competitive advantage rather than yet another factor of production. The changing management paradigm has come about mainly because of the change from the "Smokestack" era to the "Digital Era" which means that the industrial paradigm is giving way to a conception of the organization as part of a system as well as information replacing machines as the central pivot around which organizations function. In other words, the industrial organization that is characterized by the smokestack or the picture of factories and plants manufacturing goods and services has now given way to companies that use computers and the digital highway to perform their activities.

- **Consequences of the Paradigm Shift**

    This changing paradigm has been concomitant with the increasing globalization of the world economy, which has meant that corporations now operate across the world rather than in their own countries. This means that managers and management need to adopt a global outlook and at the same time execute the functions locally, which has given rise to the term, "Glocalization" that has been popularized by the noted expert, Thomas Friedman. The paradigm shift has also resulted in organizations adopting CSR or Corporate Social Responsibility and embracing diversity, which means that social and environmental concerns apart from inclusivity and tolerance are the buzzwords for managers. Further, the rise of the Knowledge Worker means that information has become the raw material that is transformed through the organizational processes rather than physical resources that are transformed through machines. Of course, this is not to say that manufacturing is dead. Rather, the point here is that the services sector that includes the IT and financial services commands the lion's share of the economy when compared to manufacturing. This has also meant that the emphasis on machine like bureaucracies has given way to systems approaches to management as the shift from manufacturing to services means that organizations are flatter, leaner, and fit than their predecessors.

- **Organizations of the Future**

The paradigm shift from the mechanistic model of organizations to the systems view has also meant that the organization of the future would be a shape-shifting one that has the ability to adapt to new market conditions quickly and rapidly than before. The advent of the internet and the increasing use of social media have meant that organizations can no longer have the luxury of taking their time to respond to market conditions and instead, the fastest, cheapest, and most innovative product wins in the market. This has again resulted in a shift from managers as bureaucrats to that of an individual who empowers and enables the workforce. The point here is that the rigid rules prescribed by management experts of the 20th century no longer work in the workplace of the 21st century where management is expected to be more innovative, inventive, and creative if it has to ensure that its companies stay ahead of the pack.

Concluding Thoughts

Finally, the paradigm shift has also meant that more women are present in the workforce and the composition of the workforce is more diverse. This means that management can no longer be an old boys club and instead has to shatter the glass ceiling to ensure that everybody has a chance to make it to the top instead of a few.